IDENTITY THEFT

Kevin Avram and Wes Boldt

Identity Theft
by Kevin Avram and Wes Boldt
Cover Design by Steve Brown
© Copyright 2006 by Kevin Avram and Wes Boldt, all rights reserved, including translation.

Printed in the United States of America

ISBN 1-886296-40-5

For additional Christian book titles or to order copies of this publication see Arrow Publications at: www.arrowbookstore.com. The text of chapter six from this publication, "The Heart Identity of a Son or Daughter," in its entirety, is contained in an inexpensive compact volume titled *The Will or The Way*. It may be obtained through Arrow Publications or your local Christian book store. For larger volume bulk orders please contact Foundations of Purpose International using the contact information provided on the back page.

"The only book that should ever be written is one that flows up from the heart, forced out by the inward pressure."

"If the reader of a [Christian] book should discover anything really new, he is in conscience bound to reject it, for whatever in religion is new is by the same token false."

"The worst thing a book can do for a Christian is leave him with the impression that he has received from it anything really good; the best it can do is point the way to the good he is seeking. The function of a good book is to stand like a signpost directing the reader toward the Truth and the Life. That book serves best which early makes itself unnecessary, just as a signpost serves best [when] it is forgotten, after the traveler has arrived safely."

A. W. Tozer, *The Divine Conquest*

Contents

TABLE OF CONTENTS

Part One

Don't Waste Your Sorrows

Kevin & Becky

After nearly 20 years of intense church involvement, based on everything Becky and I knew, we should have been living full Christian lives. We had spent hundreds of hours in Bible classes, attended church seminars and leadership conferences, led weekly prayer meetings, and taught classes on Sundays. I had been a church board member and director of an evangelical school association. Both of us had been employed in church or church-related organizations. Our three children had received their elementary and high school education at private Christian schools.

When we first came to faith in Christ as newlyweds, Becky and I had been emotional and social cripples. We had both grown up in dysfunctional homes without a solid emotional or social connection to even a single member of our immediate families. When we received new life in Christ, fellow churchgoers became our surrogate family. The church building and the activity within it fed the deep emotional and social deficiencies that had characterized our lives—deficiencies that led us to think and behave like orphans.

In the congregational tradition of which we were a part, commitment to the local church was not only taught, it was considered equal to one's relationship with God. If you loved God, you went to church. If you had a relationship with God, you participated in the activities and functions of the church. If you wanted to know God in a deeper way, you went to church more often and participated in special meetings and summer camps. When we spoke of church, we thought of church culture, church buildings, church programs, and church leadership structures. But now, nearly 20 years later, we were in the midst of an identity crisis. We knew the Scriptures. We had tasted the faithfulness of God. We had learned what it meant to trust Him for groceries, finances, and health in the midst of sickness. Yet somehow, our attitude and disposition toward church seemed to be changing. In the past, our focus on church and church activities had met spiritual, social, and emotional needs. Now church seemed to be a constraint. Why the change? Had we become rebellious? Unsubmissive? Were we lacking in commitment?

As we struggled with these questions, we were also beginning to see the fruit of our years of intense church involvement in the lives of our three teenagers. Becky and I had grown up in dysfunctional families without structure; our children grew up in a *culture* of intense structure—and control. Our church, along with the elementary and high school attached to it, had taught them how to labor, ostensibly to please God and earn His favor, but at the same time, creating a situation where their sense of purpose was supposed to come from the structure and regime of church.

Meanwhile, at home, our desire to protect them from the horrendous experiences we had known made us want to control major aspects of their lives, for when mothers and fathers desire to protect their children from something, control is the easiest way, especially for parents who are immature. As our children approached adulthood, they began to question the inordinate control that characterized our church life and our relationship with them.

While this unsettledness over church and family was taking place, I was struggling on a personal level as well. As a new believer, and throughout the years we had been Christians, I had heard over and over that God had a plan for my life. I believed every word of it, which, in the end, led me away from God. I say this because I didn't know any other way to think about such a concept except through the prism of what I was *supposed to do.* I thought "God's plan for my life" was an activity or responsibility I was supposed to discover and engage in—like following a blueprint God had sketched out for me. I thought my purpose in life was to unearth His plan, then do it with all the passion and commitment I could muster. After a season of seeking God's direction, through a series of unexpected events I felt God leading me to become involved in public policy issues, working with member organizations and lobby groups.

I loved working with lobby groups and, believing God had led me into that career path, I quickly concluded that I had finally found His plan for my life. So strongly did I believe this that with boundless passion, backed by a strong sense of commitment, I even gave talks about the value of purpose, the power of passion, and what it means to stand up for what is right. I became a crusader. I established an organization that quickly grew to nearly 100 contract agents, employees, and advisors working out of six regional offices scattered across thousands of miles. Backed by a multi-million dollar budget, the organization was in a position to *make things happen,* and often did. Our success was considerable, and people began to arrive from other parts of the world to study what we had done and figure out ways to duplicate it.

What I didn't know, and what my pride would not permit me to see, was that the single-minded pursuit of "God's plan for my life" was costing me what was integral to a healthy relationship with Him and with my family: humility and an abiding sense of dependence. I ended up in a condition where the purpose I was walking in and the good things I wanted to achieve had a greater hold on my heart than God.

Rather than finding my identity in God, I found it in my work and what I understood to be the "calling" He had for my life. At the time, I didn't know that the pursuit of purpose, no matter how noble, if conducted outside the context of humility and dependence, is the same thing as pursuing and serving a graven image or idol. In my case this was especially true, as the *image* I served literally existed in the form of a *vision* I held in my heart and mind. I was infatuated with the concept of visionaries—people who could dream big dreams and make them happen.

In many ways, the realignment the Father subsequently walked me through began during a season of ill health for my wife Becky. Like me, she had come to prize commitment, passion, and purpose, but unlike me, she couldn't find identity in such things. Instead she became alarmed by it all. Her turning point came when the Father showed her that self-sufficiency and arrogance are differing expressions of the same thing—pride. He revealed it to her one morning when she came across a man whom she knew to be struggling, and rather than responding in compassion or feeling the compulsion to pray for him, she criticized him in her heart for his inability to be self-sufficient.

The hardness of Becky's response scared her, and sensing she could do nothing to change how she was, she prayed, asking the Father to soften her. A month or two later, she was in the hospital. The pace of her life was catching up to her. Her nervous system was shutting down. She couldn't walk. The tests the hospital put her through were inconclusive, but the doctor suggested she probably had Multiple Sclerosis (MS).

The diagnosis proved wrong, and Becky eventually made a full recovery, but the process of regaining her health required her to spend many weeks flat on her back, unable to do anything, and several subsequent months recuperating. She grew keenly aware of her limitations and weakness. In the midst of this helplessness, she came to enjoy prolonged quiet times of deep intimacy with the Father. Among other things, He showed her that her true identity had nothing to do with what *she did*, but with *who she was in Him*. Speaking about this experience years later, she said:

When I got sick, Kevin and I had been believers for 16 years, and I had spent every one of those years trying to be the best wife, the best mother, and above all, the best Christian I could be. I was desperately trying to live life and raise our children in a way that did not mirror my own childhood. By the time I ended up in the hospital, I was exhausted...

Many weeks passed before Becky was able to return to church. When she did, it was all she could do to walk, but she was determined to go. Upon arrival, when asked by a woman she knew how she was doing, Becky responded by saying she was 97 percent, which was an exaggeration—a deliberate effort to be positive. The woman "tsked, tsked" her, then chided: "Now Becky, that's not faith. You should be 100 percent!" Becky was deeply hurt, not because of how the rebuke was intended to make her feel, but because what the woman had said contradicted everything the Father had been teaching her—that it wasn't her strength, but His. For months, He had been teaching her that life is in hearing Him, trusting Him, and learning how to listen to Him rather than herself. That Sunday morning experience confirmed Becky's determination to discover more fully what it meant to have a relationship with her Father. During this season of her life, she spent many hours alone with Him. Prayer became an experience of hearing the Father's voice. Also during this time, He began a 10-year process that would reveal to her what it means to have the heart attitude and identity of a Daughter, as opposed to the heart attitude and identity of a Laborer, Orphan, or Beggar. It was a pivotal point in her life, and because I am her husband, the change proved to be pivotal in mine as well.

Some time after Becky had become bedridden, God began the process that would realign my understanding of what it means to be a Christian, and the Son of my heavenly Father. I found myself in a situation where I felt I had no choice but to walk away from the organization I had birthed, nurtured, and labored over. I was heartbroken.

Within weeks, the other shoe dropped when God spoke to both Becky and me, each independent of the other, telling us to leave the institutional church. Becky was at home preparing dinner when the Holy Spirit spoke to her. I was stopped at a red light waiting to make a left turn, making my way home through traffic. We both knew what it meant to hear from God, but the instruction to pull ourselves out of the institutional church we had attended, and that had for so many years defined our lives, was not the kind of thing we would have expected the Lord to say. As a result, when I arrived home, I was somewhat uncertain how to explain to Becky what I felt the Father telling me. I had little to be concerned about. I had only said a few words when she quietly said, "I know. The Lord told me the same thing this afternoon." We both had a quiet inner knowing, accompanied by the same Scripture where God told Abraham to "go forth from your country and from your relatives... to the land which I will show you" (Gen. 12:1). Within one short season, not only had I lost the career and position I thought had been God's plan for my life, now we were being told to leave the institutional church that had been the foundation of our lives—for all our adult lives. We had nothing to go on but the inner witness of the Spirit. Becky and I questioned ourselves—many times. Our friends didn't understand. Our church leaders didn't understand. The most devastating blow of all came when one even suggested, after the culmination of a series of church-related discussions, that I was "deceived."

Isaiah 46 tells us God sees the end from the beginning. He knows the steps we need to take, which curves are ahead, and where not to go. When He led us out from all we had known and trusted, we were forced to look only to Him for direction. And once the façade of the busyness of career and church were stripped from our lives, hurts and wounds that had never been dealt with, some going back decades, demanded to be addressed. My father's suicide when I was 10 years old, Becky's father's alcoholism and abandonment of his family for long periods at a time, patterns of addiction and abuse stretching back generations in both our families, and the culture of denial and dishonesty that protected and fostered them—all these things commanded our attention.

God showed us the wounds in our hearts that had been caused by the complete lack of emotional and spiritual transparency with which we had grown up. As He began to initiate this process of healing, we began to understand the impact such things had had upon our hearts, the perspective in which we lived, and the way we had raised our children. We also came to understand the medicating and numbing effect religion and church involvement had had upon our lives. The Father showed me how much of a controller I had been, even in the midst of telling myself I was doing good things.

For a period of seven years, Becky and I experienced a kind of spiritual wilderness or desert. Then God led us into a literal desert. We had often discussed the possibility of living in Arizona, but for some reason, we never really believed it possible. We loved the Southwest and often pulled our little camper trailer to the desert when we took our vacation in the winter. One day, I simply walked in our front door and suggested we really do it—that we move to Arizona. As it turned out, Becky had been reading in Mark 6:31 where Jesus says, "Come apart into a desert place and rest awhile" (KJV). In the passage, Jesus had taken the disciples away to be alone in the desert with Him. We realized He was going to do the same with us.

During that first year in Arizona, I would go for long walks, using the time to pray that God would align the issues of my heart and life. Also during this time, God was depositing rich things into Becky's life. He was teaching her more about the attitudes of the heart and how they shape identity. She pondered these things, praying that God would realign my life, giving me the heart identity of a Son.

At the end of our first year in Arizona, Wes's email arrived. He had learned from his brother, an old friend of mine, that we were living in Mesa. Wes emailed me, explaining that he and his wife, Mary, were wintering in the Phoenix area. He suggested we meet for coffee at Starbucks around Shea Boulevard and 92nd Street. It had a patio area where we could sit, sip, and chat. People transplanted from the prairie region of Canada love to frequent such places in the middle of January.

Wes and I didn't know each other well. Twenty years earlier, we had briefly attended the same church, and on one occasion, shared a meal. Even so, our initial visit lasted several hours. Thereafter, two, three, and even four times a week, we would get together to talk about everything we could think of, but mostly God and church. From day one, there was a willingness in each of us to be transparent with the other about virtually everything in our lives—needs, family secrets, woundedness, pride, and wrong decisions. Neither of us had an agenda. Neither of us had anything to prove.

In the ensuing months, it became apparent that God was using our regular coffee talks to unfold something in Wes and me that was His. We would walk away from our two- and three-hour sessions fully aware we had been taught by the Spirit. Our conversations were drawing out of us things deposited by God—things we didn't even know were there.

Wes & Mary

For Mary and me, November 13, 1997, was a turning point in our lives. That's the day I took the check to the bank. Our business of 26 years had been sold, and for the first time in my life, when I got up in the morning, I had no place to go. At one time I would have craved such an opportunity, but when you're a person whose identity is derived from what you do, idleness quickly grows old, and even becomes something to fear.

From as early as I can remember, I had wanted to be a businessman. But my understanding of what it meant to love and please God was very narrow and did not include being in business. My family's religious tradition was rigid. Before moving to the city where I received most of my education, we had lived in a tiny farm community in the east central region of Saskatchewan, Canada. We were part of a tradition so strict a relative of mine had been ostracized by the church for having a radio. The men sat on one side of the sanctuary, the women on the other. Card playing—even the benign variety like Crazy Eights and Go Fish—was thought to be a one-way ticket to hell. And because the English-speaking farmer who lived across the road from the church building couldn't speak the language we thought would be spoken in heaven—German—he was unwelcome at the services.

Mary grew up in a mainline evangelical denomination, and around the time of our marriage, I began to attend the same congregation that she did. But in my heart, I still kept to the same legalistic path I had followed in my childhood. Wanting to please God, and believing it to be my duty, I decided I would have to go to Bible school and become a pastor. Fortunately, that's when Stanley Tam, President of United States Plastics and author of the book *God Owns My Business*, came to speak in our city. At the time, Stanley was well known for his enormous wealth and for the huge sums of money he poured into ministry and Christian service projects.

Country bumpkin that I was, I had heard of millionaires and even multi-millionaires, and sometimes wondered what it might be like to meet or see one. In part, this probably explains why I was unimpressed when I first laid eyes on Stanley Tam. I figured his gray suit looked too rumpled and crinkled to be worn by a millionaire. He seemed quiet and humble, rather than assuredly self-confident. In my youthful immaturity, I had no idea what to expect a multi-millionaire to look like, but it certainly wasn't a humble man in an unpressed suit. I had a lot to learn.

Stanley spoke for an entire series of weekend meetings. It was a weekend that changed my life. He told the story of his life and wealth, acknowledging that the wealth wasn't his, but God's. He said whether we are employed inside the church or outside the church, we are each ministers. It doesn't matter if a person is a student, dentist, floor sweeper, or businessman—each one has a different job description, and most assuredly, the person outside the formal structure of church has a closer connection with the community. Back then, I wouldn't have known how to explain the impact of his messages, or of his life upon mine. But I now know he was speaking to my heart and that I was listening with my heart. I was changed and redirected.

On Sunday evening, the last service Stanley preached, there was an altar call for people open to God's purpose. Stanley said he would pray for those who came forward. Mary and I, less than two years married, went forward together. When we did, almost immediately, Stanley made his way off the platform and walked directly over to where we were standing. He said he believed God wanted us in business. I was so relieved I could have kissed him. Business was in my heart, and his words affirmed that I would not have to follow through on my reluctant decision to attend Bible school and become a pastor. I was euphoric, feeling as if I had found myself and God's purpose for me. On the day I deposited the check from the sale of our business, the ministry of Stanley Tam was roughly 30 years in the past. In partnership with my brother, I had spent 26 of those years building a successful printing company. We had worked hard, and God had blessed us.

During all the years we were in business, Mary and I had been part of the same church. She had been involved in many ways, including the worship ministry. She loved to sing and lead worship. For more than 20 years, I had served on the elders' board, including a stint as treasurer during a major relocation-building project. That was followed by several years as board chairman. We gave a lot of time to the church. Following Stanley Tam's lead, we also gave a lot of money. We were as busy as we knew how to be, trying to please God by building His church, running a business, and raising a family.

I was living on autopilot during those years. This is the only way I know how to explain why I didn't pause for even a second to consider that there might be a difference between the church as an institution and the church as a Christ-centered body of believers. I was so confident and ambitious that I didn't have time for the more organic aspect of church, including relationships. I was interested solely in building the institution. I figured if God could be pleased with a successful large church, how might He feel if we could build a successful mega-church?

But the Holy Spirit had more to do in our lives. He had already begun to work in Mary's heart, preparing her for what lay ahead. Two years before the business was sold, Mary, who worked as our corporate financial administrator, would often come home at the end of the day asking, "Is this all there is to life?" Though I didn't understand Mary's unsettledness at first, I came across Bob Buford's book *Half Time,* a book that considers the very real distinction between *success* and *significance.* God used it to prepare my heart, and I, too, began asking: "Is this all there is to life?"

Shortly thereafter, in a move we would never have anticipated, our largest competitor offered to buy our business. We were ready. Little did Mary and I realize that the sale of our business would force a realignment in almost every aspect of our lives, including our understanding of church and what it means to live with the heart identity of a Son and Daughter. In retrospect, I see that God had to remove us from predictably familiar circumstances and the idol of *busyness* we so dutifully worshiped before we would let Him touch the real issues of our hearts. He wanted to teach us, but He had never before had our undivided attention.

With the removal of the business from our lives, the basis upon which I had found my identity and understood my purpose was no longer valid. My role as a check writer to the church had also stopped, meaning I was about to discover how intricately my ability to give financially had influenced, and at times even defined, my sense of identity.

Shortly after the business was sold, Mary and I decided to spend a few months at our condo in Arizona. We packed up and headed south. With the change of scenery, I briefly enjoyed a season of idleness, but after a few rounds of golf, it was obvious I wouldn't be joining the PGA tour. What was I to do? Though Mary and I had begun attending a good Bible-teaching church in the Scottsdale area, and were enjoying the fellowship and the things we were learning, I still craved a better understanding of my identity.

I had no choice but to cry out to God. In response to my cry, God began to teach me in two areas. The first was regarding spiritual gifts, especially the motivational gifts of Romans 12. The second was the difference between being a member of His body, the church, and belonging to or holding a position in a religious institution.

I learned God had hardwired certain gifts right into my being—gifts that were functioning at every waking moment, not only within the context of church. While my identity could only be found in Him, my purpose, in part, was to express the giftedness He had given. Equally important was how the Father taught me the difference between expressing His life through my identity as His Son, and me striving as a Laborer to accomplish some religious goal within the context of the institutional church.

As the Father taught me about heart attitude and motivational gifts, I began to see past experiences in a new light, especially things that had occurred when I was a church board member—how badly I had misunderstood some people and situations, how pridefully and single-mindedly I had assumed things about people and their motives. I realized how foolish I had been to derive self-worth and identity from my status as a business owner and position in the church. Living in the Arizona desert, I didn't have either. And every time a new person I met asked, "What do you do?" I wanted to run away. I didn't have an answer. I didn't have a business card, a title, or an activity with which I could identify. I felt absolutely naked. I had the heart attitude and identity of a Laborer, but there was no labor for me to engage in.

Mary and I had sacrificed endless hours and large sums of money for our church, yet it was in our desert wilderness experience that the true nature of our relationship with the institutional aspect of church was revealed. We discovered that the basis for most of our relationships had been work- and church-related rather than personal. The men I had worked with on the elders' board disappeared out of my life. I remember how happy I was the night one of them called on the phone, and my deep disappointment when I realized the only reason for the call was an appeal for funds. Was my worth as a man and church member derived solely from what I could contribute to the institution? Was the glue that had previously held all our relationships together only the institution, its goals, and our giving?

Eventually, I realized that after 30 years of adult living and more than 20 years as a church board member at a mainline evangelical church, I didn't even know what church was, and worse, I didn't even know who I was.

As Mary and I slowly began to gain a new understanding of what the Father was working in us, other obstacles arose. We naively expressed what we were learning to people we thought to be friends, only to find ourselves rejected. Our perspective and their perspectives were no longer the same. We were shunned by some, accused by others. At times, the pain and loneliness seemed unbearable.

Mary was also going through deep internal struggles. After the company was sold, she too realized how much her identity had been rooted in the business. In addition, God had begun to reveal areas in her life He wanted to deal with, if she would let Him. She had enrolled in a Bible study at our Scottsdale church called "Breaking Free" by Beth Moore. Through this study, God began an intensely painful process of excavation in her heart, showing her unresolved and unsettled issues that she had been accumulating—the impact legalism had had upon her life, the unmet desire she had always carried for more children, her loneliness, and the childhood abuse she had experienced at the hands of a family friend she should have been able to trust. In addition, she was still trying to grapple with the fact that her elderly father, whom she dearly loved, and who had served God all his life, fell from the top of an escalator at a shopping mall and died without her saying goodbye to him.

The final straw fell when we learned that our youngest son, now an adult, was going through a deep internal struggle largely due to the fact that he had been sexually abused as a child by a former neighbor. When we found out, we were devastated. Finally, Mary lost it. I well remember the day she stood in our kitchen, screaming that she was going to end her misery by ending her life. It was simply a matter of when and how. The honesty of her cry scared both of us so deeply that we cast ourselves upon God. There was nothing left within us to rely upon. He led Mary to seek the assistance and ministry of a wise Christian woman and in the ensuing months and years, He has proved Himself faithful.

Kevin Avram and I had met 20 years earlier when we both lived in the same western Canadian city. I didn't realize he was living in Arizona, just a few miles from our condo, until my brother mentioned it one day and passed along Kevin's email address. A few days later, we met for coffee. When I first laid eyes on Kevin, not having seen him for a good many years, I realized I was looking at a deeply wounded man. Clearly, the road he'd been walking was bumpy, riddled not just with potholes, but large chasms. He now tells me that at the time, I looked the same.

Kevin and I spoke about God, church, deep personal conflicts, doubts, fears, and uncertainties. After that initial meeting, we got together on a regular basis, and found there were no boundaries to what we discussed. Hurtful childhood events, the struggles of our children, family secrets—nothing was out of bounds or off limits. Both of us possessed a willingness to be absolutely vulnerable with the other, neither of us fearing what the other might think. We sensed that the hand of God was on our relationship and in our coffee talks.

By the time we met for that first coffee talk, I had spent several years learning about and prayerfully considering spiritual gifts. Kevin had spent 20 years working with non-profit organizations, much of it in a consulting capacity. He had developed a keen understanding of the subtle but profound distinction between such things as vision and ambition, values and purpose, activity and identity. We soon discovered the Holy Spirit had taught each of us things that complemented what He had taught the other. The day I suggested that the reason Kevin felt awkward and out of place in many social situations is in large part due to the type of gifting God had given him, the lens through which he saw the world became a little clearer. The day he suggested that no matter how committed, passionate, or well-meaning a church leader like me might have been, a vital distinction must be made between ambition and God-given vision, the lens through which I saw the world became a little clearer. That's how our coffee talks went. Kevin talked about why a leadership structure has to distinguish between identity and activity and what happens if it doesn't. I spoke of internal motivation and God-given gifts that are hardwired into us at birth. There were days one of us would say something or express an idea we both knew to be true, but had been unaware we knew. The Father was teaching us.

After many gallons of coffee and hundreds of hours of conversation, it dawned on us that almost everything we had discussed, and that the Father had shown, was related to identity, the expression of identity, and how the quest to establish an identity on the basis of our own self-sufficiency displaces the real thing in both people and churches. It is nothing less than identity theft.

Part Two

Identity Myths

Limitations of Language

L inguists understand the limitations of language and know there are times when it is very difficult for a word or concept to cross a language barrier, sometimes impossible.

For example, every Bible translator has to deal with the Hebrew word *kebes* and the Greek word *amnos,* both meaning "lamb." John the Baptist declares Jesus to be the Lamb of God (John 1:29), and the word lamb appears over and over throughout Scripture. But what if the translator is working in a remote tribal setting where there are no lambs? People living in such a place would have no understanding of a lamb and no indigenous word available to describe it. As far as they are concerned, lambs do not exist.

Translators also know it is not unusual to find instances where a particular word will translate from one language to another, yet upon translation, lack precision. Greek to English is an example.

In English we say, "God loves me," "I love popcorn," and "I love my friend Sally." We speak of husbands and wives who "make love," parents who "love their children," and politicians who "love the perks of office." English speakers use a single word to describe each of these situations, even though the *love* being talked about arises from different motives, means something different, and exists in entirely different contexts. The Greek language uses five words. Each is precise and conveys a very different idea. The words are *agape, phileo, thelo, eros*, and *storge.*

Agape is pure and selfless love that originates solely in the character and disposition of the person who loves. It has nothing to do with the disposition of the one who is loved. *Phileo*, often called brotherly love, is an expression of personal affection. It is love that finds attraction and friendship in another person and receives the same in return. *Thelo* is an intense desire to do something, such as the Pharisees who loved positions of prominence. *Eros* is sensual and sexual love. *Storge* is the unique kind of love that exists between parents and children, soldiers in trenches, and similar family-like situations.

The peculiarity of the English language is that without introducing distinctions made by the Greeks, a discussion about love lacks precision, and can even be confusing.

The English language is also wanting when it comes to discussing identity. This linguistic haziness has led more than a few people to conclude that their identity is the same as their appearance or behavior. In other instances, people think identity is a healthy sense of personhood derived from an abundance of possessions, social position, or individual achievement.

Collectively, these assumptions form what are called the "identity myths."

Identity Myth #1: Appearance Equals Identity

This means of identification, that appearance equals identity, is useful when we apply it to objects, but the minute we apply it to people, reality is obscured. In people, identity and appearance are never the same. Appearance can reflect things about a person's inner life; but even then, what is echoed in the face or conveyed by body posture is not the same as identity.

God Himself refutes this appearance-is-the-same-as-identity myth in I Samuel 16, where the story is told of David's appointment as King of Israel. In verse one, God says He has chosen a new king from among the sons of Jesse and instructs Samuel to make his way to the village of Bethlehem to anoint him.

At the first meeting between Jesse and Samuel, Eliab, Jesse's older son and David's older brother, is present. When Samuel sees this impressive-looking fellow, his immediate reaction is to assume Eliab will be king. In response to Samuel's unspoken thought, God speaks to him saying, "Do not look at his appearance or the height of his stature, because I have rejected him; for God sees not as man sees, for man looks at the outward appearance, but the Lord looks at the heart." (I Sam. 16:7)

The truth God spoke to Samuel, and to each of us through the recorded Scriptures, is that identity and appearance are not the same. Appearance is a physical phenomenon. Identity is of the heart. Jesus echoes this in John 7:24, where He tells us not to "judge according to appearance, but judge with righteous judgment." He pointed out over and over to His disciples, to the Pharisees, and to the crowds who followed Him, that identity is of the heart, and that the issues of life flow from the heart. (Matt. 5:8; Matt. 12:34; Matt. 15:8; Luke 6:45; Prov. 4:23)

Identity Myth #2: Behavior Equals Identity

If a driver obeys speed laws not because he wishes to drive responsibly or has concern for fellow motorists, but because he fears receiving another traffic ticket, his behavior has nothing to do with his true desire. How he would drive if he knew, beyond a doubt, there were no policemen around and no chance of getting a ticket is the real measure of what is inside of him. Every one of us is the same. The only accurate barometer of our condition is how we behave if no one is watching and there is absolutely no chance of getting reprimanded or even found out for what we might do.

In Bible days, this false assumption that behavior is the same as identity was the foundation of a Pharisee's life. The Pharisees studied the Scriptures, regularly attended religious services, prayed, tithed, and gave alms to the poor. Yet to their faces, Jesus and John the Baptist called them a brood of poisonous snakes. (Matt. 3:7; Matt. 23:33)

Jesus and John understood that the Pharisees' belief that they could change their identity by changing their behavior poisoned their minds, separated them from God, and led them to make false conclusions about other people, their sect, and themselves. Jesus consistently ignored their behavior, telling them, "God knows your hearts" (Luke 16:15), affirming that identity and the issues of life flow from the heart. (Prov. 4:23)

Identity Myth #3: Possessions Equal Identity

Living in a nation or culture that prizes financial success means people more easily fall into the trap of associating their identity with their possessions. The news media does it all the time. For example, people like Bill Gates and the billionaire heirs of Sam Walton, founder of the WalMart Empire, are not known for the way they treat their children after a long hard day at work—they are famous because of their wealth. That these wealthy people may or may not be good parents or marriage partners has little impact on what most people see as their true identity—their money.

The same considerations apply to non-billionaires. There are all kinds of men and women with all kinds of incomes who associate their earnings with their identity. They conclude that a bigger house in a better neighborhood changes who they are.

This is an error that Jesus warned against. He pointed out that even when a person has an abundance of possessions, to associate them with identity is wrong:

> Someone in the crowd said to Him, "Teacher, tell my brother to divide the family inheritance with me." But [Jesus] said to him, "Man, who appointed Me a judge or arbitrator over you?" Then [Jesus] said to them, "Beware, and be on your guard... for not even when one has an abundance does his life consist of his possessions." And He told them a parable, saying, "The land of a rich man was very productive. And he began reasoning to himself, saying, 'What shall I do, since I have no place to store my crops?' Then he said, 'This is what I will do: I will tear down my barns and build larger ones, and there I will store all my grain and my goods. And I will say to my soul, "Soul, you have many goods laid up for many years to come...."' But God said to him, 'You fool! This very night your soul is required of you; and now who will own what you have prepared?'" (Luke 12:13-20)

Even some who will readily agree that their income and the size of their house are not a reflection of who they are can be captivated by this myth. They may accumulate a hoard of *stuff*, cluttering their homes and their lives with childhood memorabilia—their favorite books, films, or music, and keepsakes passed down from one generation to the next.

Their homes become museums of their lives, and each item in them, they believe, embodies some aspect of who they are. The unspoken assumption is that the sum total of their *stuff* makes up their identity. This explains the devastation they feel if their house is burned down, or destroyed in a flood or hurricane. Though they have escaped alive with their families unharmed and safe, they experience a devastating sense of loss because the objects they accumulated, and from which they derived their sense of identity, are gone.

> But the worries of the world... and the desires for other things enter in and choke the word. (Mark 4:19)

Identity Myth #4: Status Equals Identity

If a man comes into your assembly with a gold ring and dressed in fine clothes, and there also comes in a poor man in dirty clothes, and you pay especial attention to the one who is wearing the fine clothes, and say, "You sit here in a good place," and you say to the poor man, "You stand over there, or sit down by my footstool," have you not made distinctions among yourselves, and become judges with evil motives? But if you show partiality, you are committing sin. (James 2:2-4,9)

Although many people regularly show preference to one another on the basis of status, unconsciously concluding that status is a reflection of identity, it's interesting to see that Scripture condemns not just the practice of partiality but the very idea. That a man may be, or has been, President of the United States, Secretary General of the United Nations, or head of a Fortune 500 company does not change the impartiality with which the Father judges people, hears their prayers, and considers their ways. God is not a respecter of persons. (Acts 10:34; Rom. 2:11)

Part Three

Road Maps for Life

Road Maps for Life Are Called Paradigms

Most of us have heard someone say about another person that he's "stuck in the past" or "locked in a time warp." They usually mean that the person is using old information and, in many instances, information that is no longer valid or reliable as the basis for making decisions. Using a 30-year-old map of a rapidly-growing city to find a street or subdivision that didn't exist 30 years ago won't work.

In his book, *Changing on the Inside*, author John White refers to psychiatrist Scott Peck's explanation of road maps that enable us to find our way through life. He writes:

Peck says we create faulty "maps" of reality. These maps contain our basic understanding of reality, which we use to navigate through life. According to Peck, we create our maps through our contacts with other people, books, the media, and by interacting with reality. Our sources are all in some measure distorted, and our perception of them is likewise distorted.... We therefore need to correct our maps year by year, as we face the truth about ourselves and the world around us.... As Peck puts it, "The process of making revisions is painful, sometimes excruciatingly painful." As a result, many of us grow tired of the pain of updating our map. We give up our quest for understanding and content ourselves merely with owning our own map. Some people give up in their teens and remain content with an adolescent view of life. Others hang on to middle age: "Their maps are small and sketchy, their views of the world narrow and misleading. By the end of middle age most people have given up the effort. They feel certain that their maps are complete and their [personal world view] is correct (indeed even sacrosanct), and they are no longer interested in new information."

Once this happens we tend to get defensive about our maps. Should anyone challenge their accuracy, we become disturbed. Arguments… which challenge our view of life make us afraid. "We may denounce… new information as false, dangerous, heretical, the work of the devil. We may actually crusade against it, and even attempt to manipulate the world so as to make it conform to our view of reality."[1]

The road maps Peck is talking about are actually called paradigms. A paradigm (*pair-ah-dime*) is a way of looking at things. It is a pattern, example, or model by which we evaluate what we see and reach conclusions about it. Whether we realize it or not, each of us lives in a paradigm. Each of us lives with assumptions about people, our own lives, God, church, and dozens of other aspects of our existence. By these assumptions, true or false, we understand things and make choices. They are the basis by which we live.

Where these paradigms come from and why we have them is something we will look at in the following chapter, but for now, the important thing is to realize that they exist, and to understand how the paradigm in which each of us lives shapes the way we see the world.

. . . .

Paradigm Shift: Swiss Watchmaking

The quickest and easiest way to convey the nature of a paradigm is to look at the way technology changes reality for a business or industry, and consider that the same principle applies to our own lives.

Back in the early 1960s, the Swiss watchmaking industry was at the top of its game.[2] It had more than 65 percent of unit sales in the world market for wristwatches and took home more than 80 percent of the industry's profit. Industry executives were confident about the future, the role they would play in that future, and their ability to make sound decisions. Their perception was based on every lesson they had ever learned about the manufacture, distribution, and marketing of watches.

At the time, wristwatches were the same size as they are today, but the inner workings were quite different. Watches were tiny machines manufactured and assembled by skilled craftsmen who used meticulous care and precision parts. Components included miniature steel springs, carefully engineered little gears, and manual winding devices.

The beginning of the end of Switzerland's dominance of the industry occurred in the late 1960s when researchers met with a group of Swiss executives to demonstrate the world's first quartz watch. The executives examined it, held it in their hands, listened to hear if it ticked, thought about it, and then, based on everything they understood to be true, rejected an invitation to utilize the microchip in their manufacturing process.

The executives didn't understand that the basis for evaluating everything about their industry, including capital investment, labor, retail marketing, and even their own jobs, would be changed by that microchip.

Unlike the Swiss, executives at the Seiko Corporation didn't view future possibilities through the prism of what took place in the past. The result was that Seiko, along with several other companies, embraced the new technology, and from that day forward, the paradigm for the profitable mass production and marketing of wristwatches has been based on the microchip.

The Swiss industry never recovered, and today there are few people under the age of 40 who have heard of "Swiss timing." Ironically, the electronic quartz movement was developed at a research institute in Neuchatel, Switzerland.

Paradigm Shift: Zeroes and Tomcats

One of the most strikingly visual depictions of a paradigm shift is portrayed in a Kirk Douglas movie called *The Final Countdown*.[3] Douglas stars as Captain Yelland, senior commander of the *USS Nimitz*, a modern, radar-equipped, nuclear-powered aircraft carrier stacked with supersonic jet fighters and high-tech weaponry. Due to a freak electrical storm, Yelland's entire ship and crew are transported back in time to December 1941, just as the Japanese are about to attack Pearl Harbor.

Finding that his ship is 280 miles west of Pearl Harbor on December 6th, 1941, with a huge Japanese naval task force approaching, Yelland launches a couple of jet aircraft (Tomcats) to monitor two Japanese fighters that are acting as pathfinders. The Japanese airplanes (Zeroes) are piston-driven, gas-fueled, and without radar. They cruise at just over 200 miles per hour. Their task is to destroy any small ships, including civilian yachts with radios, that could warn Pearl Harbor of the approaching armada.

With a top speed in excess of Mach 2 (twice the speed of sound), the *Nimitz*'s sleek jets circle around and introduce themselves to the Japanese fighters from behind. They blow past the Japanese pilots who are traveling with open cockpits, then execute a maneuver that brings them back to the Japanese planes where they literally fly circles around them.

The Japanese pilots are baffled by what is going on, but one of them still makes a foolish attempt to engage the Tomcats. The first Tomcat downs one of the Japanese planes, which crashes into the water. Using a sidewinder missile, the second Tomcat obliterates the other Zero, killing the pilot.

The pilot of the plane that crashed into the water survives. As he is bobbing up and down in the ocean, trying to comprehend the incredible machines that killed his partner and shot him out of the sky, he catches sight of a *Nimitz*-dispatched helicopter. He has never seen such a machine. It arrives overhead, seemingly stops in midair, and lowers an electronic winch. After hauling him out of the ocean, the giant upside-down eggbeater returns to the *Nimitz* where the bewildered pilot disembarks. He is then escorted across a massive flight deck bristling with radar towers, sophisticated weaponry, and an array of supersonic jet fighters.

An hour earlier, this man believed the power of the Japanese naval task force to be unassailable. It made him feel strong, proud, and invincible. Standing on the flight deck of the *USS Nimitz,* surrounded by aircraft that travel more than twice the speed of sound, capable of firing precision missiles from miles away, the captured pilot realizes that not a single Japanese airplane about to attack Pearl Harbor will get near the place.

For the Japanese pilot, the existence of the *Nimitz* and the technology it carried changed the paradigm for armed conflict and the basis upon which the Japanese must measure military strength.

Paradigms in the Lives of Individual Christians

For Swiss watchmakers and the Japanese pilot in the preceding examples, the paradigm by which they lived was the way they understood the world. When the paradigm changed, that world was turned upside down, and the assumptions by which they had lived their lives were suddenly overthrown. In the case of the Swiss, who could not see that the shift had occurred, they lost their position as the leaders of the watchmaking industry, for reasons which were, no doubt, completely bewildering to them. In the case of the pilot, who was confronted with visual evidence of the change, he lost his identity as a member of an unassailable military force that was about to dominate the Pacific.

We all live within paradigms, including the paradigm that shapes the way we understand God. If our paradigm changes, God doesn't change or alter His opinion about what is real—we do. After the Holy Spirit illuminates our hearts and gives us a new and better understanding, we no longer see with the same eyes or measure with the same criteria. The road map by which we understand our relationship with God is changed.

This is what happened to Job. In the first part of Job 42, speaking to the Lord, Job says, "I have heard of you by the hearing of the ear; but now my eye sees you; therefore I retract, and I repent in dust and ashes." Job's paradigm had changed. His repentance occurred because rather than clinging to his old understanding, he responded in humility to a new and more precise understanding of God, revealed by the Holy Spirit.

Jesus talked about paradigms in chapter nine of Matthew's gospel when He spoke of the difference between new and old wineskins:

> No one puts a patch of unshrunk cloth on an old garment; for the patch pulls away from the garment, and a worse tear results. Nor do people put new wine into old wineskins; otherwise the wineskins burst, and the wine pours out and the wineskins are ruined; but they put new wine into fresh wineskins, and both are preserved. (Matt. 9:16,17)

Scripture is brimming with examples of people with different paradigms and stories of how they clashed. An example of this is when Nicodemus approached Jesus in John 3. Jesus spoke of the work of the Holy Spirit and being born from above. Nicodemus listened and asked, "How can these things be?" Jesus was talking about a work of the Spirit. Nicodemus thought he was talking about re-entering his mother's womb.

Nicodemus was a Pharisee. He was a man of the law who saw God as a judge, and as such, he had spent his life working to emulate righteousness. This was his paradigm. Jesus was a Son who saw God as His Father. This was His paradigm. You can see why there was confusion, for though Nicodemus and Jesus spoke of the same God, so long as Nicodemus kept trying to understand on the basis of his own paradigm, he could not comprehend what Jesus was saying.

Proverbs 3:5 says we are not to "lean on our own understanding," for when we do, we trust a paradigm fashioned by our own thinking. We limit the work of God in our lives, for "as the heavens are higher than the earth, so are His ways higher than our ways and His thoughts higher than our thoughts." (Is. 55:9)

Prisoners of Paradigms

Consider the Swiss watchmaking executives referred to earlier in this section. They wanted to maintain their position as the leading manufacturers and distributors of watches. But no matter how much they wanted this, the limitations of their paradigm prevented them from understanding that the new technology was the only way this could be possible. Though they had free will, their will was a prisoner of their paradigm, and when presented with information that would revolutionize their industry and put most of them out of business, the exercise of their will still had to take place within the boundaries that defined that paradigm.

It is the same for all of us. The will is free only within the confines of context, much the same way a football or hockey game can only take place within defined boundaries, be it painted lines or painted boards. Beyond the boundaries, there is no game. For Christians, the boundary that constrains our will is our heart identity, which we will look at in the following section. In brief, this heart identity is a composite of two things: the attitude of our heart—either pride or humility—as a response to truth, and the paradigm that is immediately formed toward the circumstances of life as a result of that response. How this paradigm is formed and its role in shaping a person's outlook and life choices will also be examined in the following section.

Part Four

Identity Is of the Heart

Heart Attitude + Paradigm = Heart Identity

Heart:

> a) essence, core, the central, vital, or main part;
> b) the human heart considered as the center or
> source of identity.

Identity:

> a) sameness;
> b) being the same as who or what we identify with.

"Out of the heart flow the springs of life." Prov. 4:23[4]

To understand the two components that make up your identity, think of epoxy. Most people think of epoxy as a glue or perhaps the liquid metal repair product sold at auto parts stores and elsewhere under the trade name JB Weld.

An epoxy is made from two things—a bonding agent and a hardener. In the case of a retail product like JB Weld, it comes packaged in two tubes. One tube contains epoxy resin, and the other contains hardener. When mixed together in equal portions, you get a paste that stays pliable for about thirty minutes. Within a matter of hours, a chemical reaction occurs that turns the mixture into something as hard and tough as steel—and with similar properties. It's water-proof, petroleum- chemical- and acid-resistant, withstands temperatures up to 500° F, and resists shock and vibration. It is used to fix and patch steel hulls in boats, engine blocks, and metal pipes. You can drill holes through it and pound it with a hammer. For those who understand such things, it has a flex strength of over 7,000 pounds per square inch.

Heart identity is also a composite of two ingredients. The first of these is the attitude of our heart (either pride or humility) as a response to truth. The second is the paradigm that is immediately and inevitably formed toward the circumstances of life as a result of that response.

When the attitude of our heart is pride, the paradigm that defines and shapes the way we see the world will not be of our own choosing. It will not be something we consider and select from an array of options. Instead, through an entirely unconscious process, the prism through which we see the world and reach conclusions will be imposed on us by the experiences of life with which we are most familiar, and therefore most readily identify with. We take on the heart identity of a Laborer, an Orphan, or a Beggar.

When the attitude of our heart is humility, we are positioned to take on the heart identity of a Son or Daughter. Sons and Daughters are freed from past experiences as the basis upon which to live. What they have done and where they have been no longer defines who they are. Instead, the paradigm within which they live and the prism through which they see the world is based on the identity and declarations of God. (John 8:35,36)

Our Heart's Response to Truth: Pride and Self-sufficiency or Humility

The dictionary says pride is exaggerated self-esteem, conceit, and the haughty behavior that occurs as a result. Though this is an accurate description of what pride looks like, it doesn't explain what pride actually is. Saying pride is equivalent to an arrogant attitude is like saying a tsunami is a huge sea wave that causes floods and kills people. This too is accurate, but knowing what tsunamis look like and how they behave doesn't explain what they are. To understand tsunamis requires familiarity with plate tectonics and conditions leading to underwater earthquakes and volcanoes. A tsunami wave is a consequence; underwater earthquakes and volcanoes are the cause.

Arrogance and conceit are also consequences. They are to pride what a tsunami wave is to an underwater earthquake. In reality, pride is the quest for an identity that is not our own. It is the decision to assume an identity rooted in events, conditions, or circumstances. It is an attitude of the heart that rejects the authority and declarations of God, and presumes we have the latitude to derive our identity from a source other than God and apart from what He declares to be true. If our heart's response to truth is pride, the paradigm through which we see the world will be rooted in a spirit of self-sufficiency, giving birth to one of three distinct heart identities. Part Five explains each of these identities in detail, but in brief, they are:

Laborer

Laborers find identity in their work, like and trust systems, and desire to emulate those who know how to "get things done" or "make it happen." They want to please God, and believe they can do this through their labor or achievement. They believe that, in the end, they will receive recognition and reward for what they do or accomplish.

Orphan

Orphans cannot find their identity anywhere. They are comfortless and have difficulty seeing where they fit. Their identity is defined by a persistent sense of need and a desire for Sonship/Daughterhood, but their heart's response of pride and ongoing tendency toward self-sufficiency keeps them from dependence on the Father.

Beggar

Like Laborers and Orphans, Beggars respond to truth in pride. They too see the world through the prism of self-sufficiency, but recognize they do not actually possess it. As such, they see the world as a collection of victims and villains, with themselves as the victims—even when they act as villains.

For the believer, there is a fourth possible heart identity, namely, **Son/Daughter**. This heart identity rests upon a foundation of grace, which is received on the basis of confessed need and humility (Matt. 5:3; I Peter 5:5; Gal. 4:1-6). Sonship/Daughterhood also brings with it a paradigm. But this paradigm is shaped by identification with God as Father, and the finding of our identity in His identity.

When we first come to Christ, each of us responds to truth in humility, simultaneously abandoning self-sufficiency and embracing dependence upon the Father. We acknowledge our need. When we continue to abide in this state of humility and dependence, rejecting self-sufficiency as the basis of maturity and growth, we walk in Sonship/Daughterhood. "Apart from me you can do nothing" (John 15:5). When we embrace the spirit of self-sufficiency as the avenue through which we experience maturity and growth, like the believers Paul rebuked in Galatians 3, our heart's response will be rooted in pride. We will reject the provision of God, and we will walk as Laborers, Orphans, or Beggars.

HEART IDENTITY SUMMARY

HEART IDENTITY	HEART'S RESPONSE TO TRUTH	SOURCE OF IDENTITY
LABORER	Pride	Work, achievement, earned position, expectation of future reward or payment for what is practiced or achieved
ORPHAN	Pride	Being comfortless, heartfelt awareness that Sonship/ Daughterhood is missing and an inability to see how it might be procured
BEGGAR	Pride	Being a victim
SON/ DAUGHTER	Humility	His or her Father

Part Five

Paradigms Rooted in
Self-sufficiency that
Steal Sonship/Daughterhood

The Laborer

Heart's Cry:

> "Recognition or favor from God is or will be owed to me because of what I bring about through self-effort, discipline, commitment, and passion."

Identity Source:

> Self-sufficiency; work, achievement, position, status, or the expectation of future reward or payment for services rendered.

Concept of God:

> Strict, demanding, showing favor to those who earn it and please Him.

Laborers are achievement-oriented and esteem self-reliance, considering it synonymous with maturity. They give honor to and receive honor from other people or from institutional systems. They have regard for titles, and when in a position of authority, unconsciously view control as a means to "achieve for God." Laborers readily adopt an institutional or religious mindset.

For men and women who are Laborers, identity is thought to be the fruit of their own effort. They long to emulate the accomplishments of others, especially those they see as great leaders or spiritual giants.

Laborers believe activity and achievement are synonymous with identity. They think knowing what someone else does (or what congregation they attend) tells them who that person actually is. In an institutional setting, Laborers unconsciously place a higher value on the institution than on the people in it. They often speak of "going to the next level" and view sincerity and passion as authenticating realities—visible manifestations of the depth of a person's commitment to God. Laborers believe human passion is the most effective means they and others like them can use to expand or accelerate that which they are constructing. This is because they view passion, commitment, and even humility (as they understand it) as commodities, the abundance of which theoretically provides them with greater leverage to "achieve for God."

Laborers have little regard for individual diversity. They believe the same maturing *system* or development *process* applies to every Christian, much the same way every elementary school student follows the same curriculum in order to graduate.

To the Laborer, public recognition from church officials or from the congregation as a whole will be remembered for months and even years to come. Laborers yearn for recognition and promotion. They believe God will be pleased with them if they do certain things and act in certain ways—displeased or indifferent if they don't.

Laborers fear sin. They fear it because in the hidden places of their heart, they know it is their alter ego. The religious and systemic mindset of a Laborer prohibits relational transparency, the absence of which acts as a barrier to protect what's wrong with them. In other words, they seek to obscure the desires and unresolved issues hidden in their hearts, and concern themselves with achievement or with the image they present, believing their behavior is the same as their identity. As a result, their alter ego actually thrives and is alive and well.

Laborers believe that if they can change their behavior, they can change their character, and by changing their character, they change their identity. They unconsciously conclude that Christianity is a character improvement program, and that the fruit of the Holy Spirit in their lives (Gal. 5:22,23) can be brought about through self-effort. They assume character can be manufactured, and that the formula for its production is roughly equal to:

Biblical Commands + Commitment + Willpower + Time = Character

What Laborers fail to understand is that character and identity are not the same thing. Character is a pattern of behavior expressed over time, viewed through the prism of morality. It most often refers to behavior that is a response to adversity and suffering, prosperity and blessing. Identity, however, has to do with the *underlying condition* that makes a person behave or respond in a certain way. It is not about what a person actually does so much as *why* a person does it.

In Philippians 3:6, Paul states that at one time he had been a man of impeccable character. Yet after he encountered Christ, he came to view it as trash or dung (Phil. 3:8 KJV). He then affirmed that his identity was no longer tied to his previous concept of character, but to Christ. (II Cor. 5:14-17; Gal. 2:20; Gal. 6:15)

The point Paul makes, and the point that Laborers miss, is that to the degree we experience dependence and death, we are able to express the character of Christ manifested in us as the fruit of the Holy Spirit. The *character* and *fruit* are not ours, they are His, and to the degree we think they are ours, we resist God.

Though it is true that Jesus said "Be perfect for the Father is perfect" (Matt. 5:48 KJV), character is not something we manufacture ourselves, nor is it practiced behavior that imitates Jesus. The WWJD (What Would Jesus Do) wrist bracelets and bumper stickers are an appealing idea, but not a biblical one. Christianity is not merely doing what Jesus would do. It is experiencing a man, Jesus Christ, and the life of that man.

Laborers in the Bible:
Job and the Prodigal Son's Older Brother

Many people think God blessed Job because of the way he responded to conflict and trial. The assumption is that Job passed some kind of test.

In fact, at the beginning of the book that bears his name, Job had the heart identity of a Laborer. Though he had lived a blessed life, he never knew God as his Father. He lived with the singular hope that if he conducted his life in the right manner, he could continually earn God's favor and blessing. He "would rise early in the morning and offer burnt offerings according to the number of them all [for each one of his children]. For Job said, 'perhaps my sons have sinned and cursed God in their hearts.' This Job did continually." (Job 1:5)

God knew Job had the heart identity of a Laborer; He wanted him to have the heart identity of a Son. To excavate Job's heart, God deliberately used Satan, allowing him to take everything from Job (Job 1:12). God's objective all along was to bless Job by dealing with the issues of his heart, for it is from the heart that the issues of life flow (Prov. 4:23). God desired that Job embrace humility in the midst of barrenness, because humility is the foundation of Sonship. (I Peter 5:5; Matt. 5:3)

To get to Job's heart took 41 chapters. In chapter 38, God began to reply to Job's demands by making demands of him in return. God's repeated questioning, and Job's inability to answer, humbled Job. His encounter with God changed his paradigm, and in chapter 42, he was finally able to declare, "Before my ears had heard of you but now my eyes see you." Job was not speaking of literal sight. He meant that in his heart, the paradigm that shaped the way he saw God had shifted. He was able to grasp the true nature of his own life, and God's disposition toward him.

After all he had been through, Job affirmed his repentance, and the repentance he spoke of was not a modification of behavior or a deliberate resolving to do better. It was a condition of his heart. A paraphrase of what Job said to the Father in Job 42:3-6, could read: "My heart has been wrong. My assumptions have been wrong. I used to talk about things and say things I didn't understand, believing they were right. I was proud. I was wrong. I repent. Please instruct me and teach me."[5] From his heart, Job was affirming the truth of Proverbs 3:5: "Trust in the Lord with all your heart, and do not lean on your own understanding."

When Job responded in humility and an abiding confession of his need, letting go of self-sufficiency, he entered into the spirit of Sonship. In the end, God didn't bless Job because he endured or earned some kind of favor or prize. It wasn't a payoff. The blessings in Job's life were the natural result of relationship—of

Sonship. Job no longer walked in self-sufficiency, fearing what God might do to him. He walked in humility and dependence, being instructed by the Father in His ways. "I will ask You, and You will instruct me" (Job 42:4), became the defining characteristic of his life. It is the same with every Son and Daughter. (Heb. 12:7)

Another example of an individual with the heart identity of a Laborer is found in chapter 15 of Luke's gospel, where we read of the older brother in the Parable of the Prodigal.

> The younger of them said to his father, "Father, give me the share of the estate that falls to me." So he [the father] divided his wealth between them [the two sons]. (Luke 15:12)

The younger brother, who begins the story with the heart identity of an Orphan (this will be explained later), hung around for a while, then headed off to find himself. While he was away, the older son, who had also received his inheritance, kept right on doing what he had done in the past—working, laboring, and trying to earn recognition from his father. Having received his inheritance, the circumstances of his life had changed, but his heart's response to truth and the paradigm that flowed from it remained unchanged. He lived with his father and had access to all his father had to give (Luke 15:31), but in his heart, he was still a Laborer.

After the younger brother "came to himself" (Luke 15:17 KJV), he returned home to be met by his euphoric father, who gave him gifts and proclaimed a celebration. When the older brother discovered what was going on, he became so enraged he wouldn't even go into the house. His response was rooted in the fact that his brother was getting for free what he, the older brother, believed should only be gained through merit. He said to his father:

"Look! For so many years I have been serving you and I have never neglected a command of yours; and yet you have never given me a young goat, so that I might celebrate with my friends." (Luke 15:29)

The father pleaded with his older son, explaining that like his brother, he had always had free access to his favor and all he could possibly offer (Luke 15:28-32), but the older brother's heart identity kept him from hearing and understanding.

The Orphan

Heart's Cry:

"I feel so alone. I feel so empty. I wish someone would rescue me. I wish someone would love me, accept me, and comfort me."

Identity Source:

Persistent sense of need: being comfortless; difficulty seeing where they fit; heartfelt awareness that Sonship/Daughterhood is missing—inability to see how it might be procured.

Concept of God:

Uncertain; compares what they experienced in the past regarding a father figure with what they hope He might be like.

Orphans are bereft of a guide or guardian. They are fatherless. Their lives are characterized by need. Because they are alone, if something is to happen or change in their lives, the act must be self-initiated. Yet, unlike Laborers who derive identity from making things happen, Orphans keep right on sensing a void in their lives even when others think they are successful. Orphans do not find identity in activity or achievement, sensing they have intrinsic value apart from such things. Unfortunately, they frequently find themselves in institutional and cultural settings governed by Laborers, which confuses them.

Laborers appear self-sufficient, and Orphans admire self-sufficiency, for they, like Laborers, equate it with maturity. But unlike Laborers, who genuinely believe their activity and accomplishments bring recognition from God, Orphans intuitively recognize the futility of seeking identity in labor. No matter how much they achieve, Orphans never feel the recognition they may receive is the same as the intimacy they crave.

Orphans struggle with the fact they have no context within which to understand what it means to be loved. They can smell what it is like, much the way a hungry man smells a flavorful meal when he walks in the house at the end of a long day, but Orphans never taste the meal. They believe God loves people, just as real-life orphans believe happy loving families exist, but they see themselves as being outside that love and unable to attain it. Because they find their identity in being an Orphan, and live in the paradigm and thinking processes of an Orphan, they tell themselves their neediness keeps them from being worthy of God's love.

In truth, the heart response of an Orphan is what separates them from God, for rather than responding in humility to their spiritual need (Matt. 5:3), which is the basis of embracing Sonship/Daughterhood, they respond in pride, attempting to erase their need either by withdrawing from others and erecting barriers to protect themselves, or by finding surrogates. Instead of abiding in God and that which He declares to be true, resulting in Sonship/Daughterhood, Orphans depend on themselves or other people. Relationships can be to Orphans what insulin is to a diabetic—they provide relief from the symptoms of their condition, their feelings of aloneness and abandonment, but only temporarily. The condition that creates these symptoms—the attitude of their heart—remains unaddressed.

Orphans in the Bible: The Prodigal Son

An example of an individual with the heart identity of an Orphan is the younger brother in the Parable of the Prodigal. The prodigal had probably been working alongside his brother, serving their father. Yet while the older son continued in his labor, never neglecting any of his father's commands (Luke 15:29), the younger son was restless, wanting more, and asked for his inheritance.

Unlike his older brother, who had the heart identity of a Laborer, the prodigal could not derive identity from his work. He craved something deeper, and probably hoped receiving his inheritance would fill the need in his life. The boys' father graciously divided his estate between them.

The younger son stayed home for a few days, his need apparently appeased, but only temporarily. Having the heart identity of an Orphan, he could find nothing to keep him at home once the joy of counting his money had passed. He had no emotional ties or identity connection to his father. Feeling he was alone, he tried to find comfort by taking what he had and going off by himself, as Orphans are inclined to do. Luke 15:13-19 tells us what happened next:

> And there he squandered his estate with loose living. Now when he had spent everything, a severe famine occurred in that country, and he began to be in need. And he went and attached himself to one of the citizens of that country, and he sent him into his fields to feed swine. And he was longing to fill his stomach with the pods that the swine were

eating, and no one was giving anything to him. But when he came to his senses, he said, "How many of my father's hired men have more than enough bread, but I am dying here with hunger! I will get up and go to my father, and will say to him, 'Father, I have sinned against heaven and in your sight; I am no longer worthy to be called your son; make me as one of your hired men.'"

In the pigpen, the prodigal saw his life for what it was, and "came to himself" (KJV). From his heart, he recognized that his life was defined by need, and also that he had a father who could meet that need. Admitting to need has a way of leveling everything in our lives. It opens doors (Matt. 5:3), and forces us to have an honest look at our hearts, how we live, and what we depend upon. It compels us to be honest.

The prodigal returned to his father in need, and in humility. He returned to a father who daily was watching the path from a distance, hoping his son would one day return. The Bible says the father ran out to meet him, rejoicing at the sight of him. He removed his son's old coat, which represented the heart attitude and paradigm that had previously governed the boy's life, and replaced it with a new robe, representing the heart attitude and paradigm of a Son.

The Beggar

Heart's Cry:
> "It's not my fault! I'm the victim here."

Identity Source:
> Being a victim; unforgiveness.

Concept of God:
> The ultimate controller; One who is distant; One to be afraid of.

Beggars believe the world is divided into only two kinds of people: victims and villains. But whether they are victims or villains, Beggars always see themselves as the victim.

Beggars believe they are not responsible for anything. Whatever is wrong with them is someone else's fault, or can be traced to some circumstance they could not control or opportunity they were denied. Beggars believe the circumstances of their life and even their own actions are the result of other people's actions and decisions, or in some cases, an act of God.

The heart identity of a Beggar is not to be confused with the disposition of a man or woman who has been wounded. Wounded people, like Beggars, have been genuinely hurt—either by circumstances or by other people. But unlike wounded Laborers, Orphans, or Sons/Daughters, the paradigm within which Beggars live is shaped by the unforgiveness associated with that hurt. Their sense of being a whole person has been corrupted or stolen from them by abuse, the dominance of an overbearing individual (usually a parent), or some other circumstance.

Wounded people want to get over their hurt. Beggars believe their hurt is a permanent part of their life. They see their lives through the prism of injustices done to them. They embrace unforgiveness and find identity in being the victim of another person's offense. Forgiveness requires humility, and the root of a Beggar's life is pride. From their hearts, Beggars harbor resentment, woundedness, and ill feelings. They nurture their loss because that sense of loss is integral to their identity.

The paradigm in which Beggars live compels them to live with pain. To cope with their misery, they readily embrace addictions. Drugs, pornography, and alcohol are common, but even ordinary things like food, chat rooms, video games, and television can become addictions to a Beggar. These things medicate and temporarily dull their sense of living a hopeless life.[6]

Beggars believe progress in their lives occurs only when someone with power or influence opens doors for them. Their disposition is one of perpetual reaction. Beggars resent correction and internalize criticism, even if the criticism is related to a system or institution of which they are a part. They see people who speak truth to them as their enemies, and often imagine offenses or criticisms where they do not exist. They find it easy to "fudge" the truth or lie if it will "soothe" a situation they find uncomfortable.

Beggars easily settle for that which is counterfeit. Coming to God and receiving all they need is a difficult concept for them to grasp. They don't believe they deserve anything. They can't believe God could possibly be any different from the villains they have known in their lives.

. . . .

Beggars in the Bible:
The Cripple of Bethesda and King Ahab

The heart identity of a Beggar is manifested in one of two ways. The first way can be seen in men and women who are victims. An example of this type of Beggar is the lame man at the Pool of Bethesda (John 5:1-9). The man had been lying by the pool for 38 years. He was alone, strengthless, and unable to imagine a future different from his past. Knowing this, Jesus walked up to him and asked: "Do you want to be made well?"

Jesus was speaking directly to the crippled man's heart. Knowing this illuminates His question, and the answer. Otherwise Jesus sounds heartless and we are left asking, "Why would He ask that? Of course he wanted to get better. Isn't it obvious? He had been lying there for almost 40 years!"

Instead of responding to Jesus with an emphatic "yes," the lame man replied: "There is no one to help me. Someone always gets in there ahead of me." His response reflected his identity. He said to Jesus: "I am a victim."

Jesus healed the man then faded into the crowd. Later on He found him in the temple and said, "See, you have been made well. Sin no more lest a worse thing come upon you." When Jesus said this, He was again speaking to the heart. When He warned the man about sin, He wasn't saying God would angrily strike him with sickness if he sinned, making him a cripple again, nor was He implying the man had been a cripple in the first place because he had done wrong. He was referring to the belief that had held the man's heart captive for so many years. He was referring to the heart identity of a Beggar that said: "I am a victim.

Nothing can ever change. Life can never get any better. Things will always be this way." Jesus was telling him that the consequences of sin will do to a man's heart what lameness had done to his body.

The second way the heart identity of a Beggar is manifested can be seen in men and women who are villains or who are in collusion with villains. Like the first type of Beggar, this second expression is also rooted in victimhood, the difference being the victim in this case is in a position of power or authority that gives amplification to their identity. King Ahab in the Old Testament is an example of this type of Beggar.

In Micah 6:16, when describing what evil is like, God refers to the "statutes of Omri" and the "works of the house of Ahab." Omri, also a king, was Ahab's father (I Kings 16:25). The Bible says Omri "did evil in the sight of the Lord and acted more wickedly than all who were before him." In this evil king's home, Ahab was raised and nurtured.

Despite the fact he was king, Ahab viewed himself as a victim. I Kings 21 gives the account of Ahab's desire to possess a vineyard that belonged to his neighbor Naboth. When Naboth refused to give up what he referred to as his ancestral inheritance, Ahab's response is revealing. The Bible says he returned to his home "sullen and vexed," lay on his bed, turned his face to the wall, and ate nothing. (I Kings 21:4)

As Ahab sulked, his wife Jezebel came to him and said, "How is it that your spirit is so sullen that you are not eating food?" Ahab explained that he was being victimized by Naboth's unwillingness to give him what he wanted. Jezebel told him not to worry. With Ahab's approval, she hatched a plan that would allow the two of them to steal Naboth's vineyard—a plan ending in Naboth's death.

As soon as Ahab learned Naboth was dead, he made his way to the vineyard to take possession. The Prophet Elijah confronted him there, rebuking him for his evil deed. Though Ahab and his wife were the villains, like all Beggars, Ahab immediately responded as a victim—calling Elijah his enemy.

Ahab saw Elijah as an enemy because Elijah confronted him with the truth. In Ahab's mind, what had happened to Naboth was justified because he (Ahab) was the victim. Naboth would not give him what he wanted. Elijah, as a Prophet of God, told Ahab the responsibility for what had happened was his. When Elijah told Ahab that God intended to destroy him and his household, Ahab responded in humility. When he did, God honored him, even speaking to Elijah about it (I Kings 21:27-29). God decided to have mercy on Ahab, saying that He would not destroy Ahab's household during his lifetime, but the new attitude of Ahab's heart did not last, and he returned to his villainous ways, having another prophet who spoke truth to him cast into prison. (I Kings 22:27)

Part Six

The Heart Identity of
a Son or Daughter

The Will or The Way[7]

At one time, Christians believed men and women were saved when they *heard* the gospel—a *hearing* that occurred with the heart rather than the ear. It came about when the Holy Spirit supernaturally awakened individual men and women from the deadness of their own spirit (John 6:44), resulting in the birth of spiritual Sons and Daughters who were born not of "blood, nor of the will of the flesh, nor of the *will of man*, but of God." (John 1:13)

In our consumer-driven society where individualism and personal choice reign supreme, this basic understanding is no longer prevalent. Instead, it is generally thought salvation occurs by an act of the human will when a person *chooses* to make a *commitment* to Christ. Salvation is equated with a deliberate action— responding to an altar call, raising a hand, signing a card, or reciting a particular prayer. "Just ask Jesus into your heart" is a well-known phrase within Protestant spheres of influence.

Bible teacher John MacArthur points out that the problem with such an idea is that it assumes salvation hinges on an act that originates in the human mind. He says these responses that so many equate with getting saved have nothing to do with salvation. Instead, they are the result of a deliberately cultivated religious invitationalism that suggests salvation hinges on the power of human *free will*. MacArthur writes:

> This emphasis is a peculiarly American phenomenon that started in the nineteenth century with a New York lawyer-turned-evangelist named Charles Finney....

> [Finney] insisted that people get saved by an act of
> sheer willpower…. Up to that time, American evangel-
> ists… believed that sinners are saved by hearing the
> message of the gospel while God the Holy Spirit awak-
> ens them from sinful deadness. But Finney took a dif-
> ferent path. He made emotional appeals and taught that
> salvation required no sovereign regeneration by God,
> but only the act of the human will. The people came
> streaming down the aisle under the force of his clever-
> ness. The vast majority of those weren't real conver-
> sions; in fact, Finney later admitted that his ministry
> produced mostly halfhearted and temporary "con-
> verts." But the spectacle of crowds surging forward
> was very convincing.[8]

There are two great tragedies brought about by this sort of invitationalism. The first is that it results in a situation where the human will is considered central to the life of the Christian, rather than the response of the heart to the Holy Spirit. The second is that it presumes salvation is a singular event that occurs at a specific point in time, which passes and becomes an experience we look back upon.

New Testament believers understood that salvation is not a past event but something constant—a condition in which we abide. This is why they referred to what we call Christianity as "the Way" (Acts 19:23). They understood that at the point of spiritual birth, God "rescued us from the domain of darkness, and transferred us to the kingdom of His beloved Son" (Col. 1:13). Yet even so, rather than thinking of salvation as a past event, they viewed it as an introduction to grace, or an introduction to the process of Sonship/Daughterhood (Gal. 4:6). Paul referred to it as the "grace in which we stand." (Rom. 5:2)

Sons and Daughters understand that being saved is something that happens every day, because the need that first brought us to the Father is ongoing. As such, we need to be saved not at one moment only, but at *every* moment. For Sons and Daughters salvation is not a past event, but a condition in which they live. They continue to walk in humility because they continue to recognize their need for God. They do not embrace self-sufficiency, but dependency.

Contemporary culture assumes that self-sufficiency is synonymous with maturity. The more you are able to control your own life, the more mature you are thought to be. But in the realm of the Spirit, the opposite is true. Maturity comes by leaning— abandoning self-sufficiency and refusing to rely upon our own initiative to make progress. Progress in the kingdom of God is not something we make or achieve, but a condition to which we submit.

In the economy of God, things are the opposite of what they are in the natural (Is. 55:9). The more you give, the more you receive (Luke 6:38). It is more blessed to give than to receive (Acts 20:35). The more you humble yourself, the more you are exalted (Matt 23:12). The more dependent you are, the more mature you are. (John 15:5)

When we first come to Christ, which begins the process of Sonship/Daughterhood, we enter not into a character improvement program, but into a state of abiding grace and blessedness.

Blessedness is the meaning of the word *beatitude*, the statements with which Jesus opened the Sermon on the Mount. In the beatitudes, Jesus was not describing the way Christians should behave in order to improve their character or please God. He was explaining the process that results in us having the heart identity of a Son or Daughter.

Poverty of Spirit

Blessed are the poor in spirit,
for theirs is the kingdom of heaven. (Matthew 5:3)

Poverty of spirit is where Sonship and Daughterhood begin. To be poor in spirit is to acknowledge we are not just spiritually poor, but bankrupt, and live in a state of constant, pressing, and unremitting need.[9] It is a condition of the heart rather than an inventory of available resources or abilities. It occurs when the Holy Spirit reveals to us that we are spiritually barren, and we acknowledge it honestly rather than fleeing from it or disguising it.

If we set about to flee, there are a few ways we can do it. One way is to deaden our senses by indulging appetites: alcohol, food, drugs, sex, or living in front of the television so a never-ending array of cable programs can cascade over our being. Another way to flee is to seek status, recognition, or affirmation of identity in the offerings of the world. "For all that is in the world, the lust of the eyes, the lust of the flesh, and the boastful pride of life, is not from the Father." (I John 2:15)

If we set about to disguise our spiritual barrenness, the instruments of choice are religious trappings. We cover ourselves with them even as Adam and Eve used fig leaves in an attempt to conceal who they really were and what they really looked like. Twenty-first century religious disguises include:

- Reliance upon our own initiative and know-how to make spiritual progress. (Phil. 3:3,6; John 8:28)

- The concept of being committed to learn about God and obey Him apart from abiding dependency. (John 15:4)
- Deliberate efforts to take the best techniques we can get our hands on to manufacture or expand that which we believe is lacking in our lives or in the church. (I Cor. 2:1-5)

When confronted with our spiritual poverty, a heart that responds by crying, "I have need" is positioned to know progress—not *make* progress, but *know* progress, for progress in the kingdom of God is not something we make, but a reality to which we submit. Confessing our need and embracing all it implies means we move within the perimeter of God's kingdom.[10] The message of the first beatitude and the foundation of Sonship/Daughterhood is: "Blessed are the poor in spirit for theirs is the kingdom of heaven."

Failure to confess spiritual need, or even to recognize it, prompted the Lord Jesus to rebuke the Church at Laodicea (Rev. 3:17,19). The Laodiceans thought they had "need of nothing." Jesus told them to repent, and it is to this group of self-sufficient believers He spoke the well-known words of Revelation 3:20: "Behold, I stand at the door and knock; if anyone hears My voice and opens the door, I will come in to him and will dine with him, and he with Me."

In Matthew 3, John the Baptist rebuked the Pharisees and Sadducees, saying they were a brood of vipers who needed to repent and flee the coming wrath. Yet after admonishing them and forcefully testifying of their spiritual need, he encountered

Jesus, who had come to the Jordan to be baptized, and immediately responded by declaring, "I have need to be baptized by You!"

Likewise Isaiah, throughout chapter five of the book that bears his name, pronounced judgment upon the unrighteous: "Woe to those who do not pay attention to the deeds of the Lord; woe to those who drag iniquity with the cords of falsehood; woe to those who call evil good; woe to those who are wise in their own eyes; woe to those who justify the wicked with a bribe." Yet after pronouncing woe upon the unrighteous, when he encountered the Lord a few verses later (Is. 6:5), Isaiah's immediate response was to pronounce woe upon himself and confess the depth of his own need:

"Woe is me! I am ruined! I am a man of unclean lips!"

Whether bishop, child, grandmother, pastor, housewife, or international evangelist, there is only one healthy and appropriate response to the starkness of our spiritual condition as revealed by the Holy Spirit. It is a resonating cry from the depths of our heart that declares, "I am spiritually impoverished. I have need."

Mourning Our Poverty

Blessed are those who mourn,
for they shall be comforted. (Matthew 5:4)

Some people puzzle over this verse. One man said every time he heard it or read it, he immediately envisioned a broken-hearted Jewish mother who had just lost a child due to illness, sitting on the side of a hill listening to Jesus. This man would then ask: "How could Jesus tell this woman she is blessed? What would make Him declare she should be happy about what happened, or suggest she will be happy about it at some future date? And what about the person who mourns a drug-addicted son, the suicide of a troubled friend, or the failed marriage of a loved one? What blessing could there be to the broken-hearted parent who mourns the rape of a daughter?"

To the natural man with a natural eye these questions seem reasonable. But as is always the case, rather than speaking of the obvious, Jesus speaks to the heart. He doesn't say we are blessed when we mourn *circumstances* that cause pain. He is saying we are blessed when we mourn the *spiritual poverty* responsible for the circumstances that cause such pain. Jesus is talking about the first beatitude. He is talking about mourning our spiritual need, our sin, and the sin of those around us.

To mourn is to be in a state of grief and distress. Mourning that has been husbanded by the Holy Spirit brings with it dependence, internal brokenness, and a heartfelt desire to see change in the conditions that cause such pain (Rom. 7:18-21). Mourning sin is the prelude to repentance, intercession, and change.

Repentance brought about by such mourning is not a redoubling of efforts to do better or the mere admission of wrongdoing. It is a realigning of what we are, in the deepest part of who we are. It is a spiritual condition that results in a broken spirit and contrite heart. And it is this condition to which the Father looks, and pays especial attention:

- I dwell on a high and holy place, and also with the contrite and lowly of spirit. (Is. 57:15)

- The Lord is near to the brokenhearted and saves those who are crushed [contrite] in spirit. (Ps. 34:18)

- A broken and contrite heart, O God, You will not despise. (Ps. 51:17)

- But to this one will I look, to him who is humble and contrite of spirit, and who trembles at My word. (Is. 66:2)

Hearing with the Heart

Blessed are the gentle [humble],
for they shall inherit the earth. (Matthew 5:5)

Pride hardens our hearts and protects what is wrong with us. Humility opens our hearts and enables what is wrong with us to be changed. Humility is the substructure upon which all virtue in our lives rests, for we are transformed and made righteous only by grace, and we receive grace when we are humble.[11] "God is opposed to the proud but gives grace to the humble." (I Peter 5:5)

Grace is not just God's way of forgiving and covering our sin. It is His promise, and the fulfilling of His promise, to do for each of us what we cannot do for ourselves.[12]

Humility prepares our minds, conditions our hearts, and enables us to live, walk, and abide as Sons and Daughters. Humility gives the Holy Spirit freedom to write the Father's ways and thoughts upon our hearts (II Cor. 3:3). It is in humility that we have fellowship with the Father and His Son Jesus Christ (I John 1:3). It is in humility that we freely rely upon the Father rather than our own understanding (Prov. 3:5). It is the humble He instructs in His ways. (Ps. 25:9)

Receiving, tasting, and enjoying the practical elements of Sonship/Daughterhood is rooted in humility.

"Truly I say to you, whoever does not receive the kingdom
of God like a child will not enter it at all." (Luke 18:17)

The Father initiates that which fosters Sonship/Daughterhood. In humility we come to possess it. To understand how this occurs, consider what author Eugene Peterson has to say about listening in the middle voice (paraphrase):

> Picture yourself in the office of a counselor. You talk at length while the counselor murmurs the sort of things counselors tend to murmur—encouraging background noises, a few "I sees," and "ummhmms." Finally, after you have spoken for a while, the counselor says, "Um, ah, it seems that what you are saying is... But wouldn't you also agree that...?"

> Now the counselor is actively giving counsel. You can respond to his counsel in one of three ways: You can let the counselor dictate a course of action and then immediately go out and do what he says. If you do, you will be acting in what is called the *passive voice*. In the passive voice, the origin of the action or activity is the counselor. Your submission is a *passive* response to it.

> If you reject his counsel and go your own way you will respond in the *active voice*. In the active voice, the source of the proposed action or activity is still the counselor. Your refusal to go along with it is an *active* response to it.

> The third alternative is to respond in the *middle voice*. In the middle voice you are neither passively pushed

along by the counselor's advice, nor do you actively resist it. Instead, you remain in a state of hearing, pondering what has been said. You cooperate. Then something happens. A light comes on and you declare, "Oh, I see what you are saying now! You may well be right, you know, I never saw that!" And you choose to embrace the advice as something you have now seen for yourself. You realize at once which course the real part of you wants to follow. That is, you realize what you want at the most fundamental part of your being.[13]

In the middle voice, the counsel has been internalized. Someone observing the situation might mistakenly conclude you are *passively* submitting to the counselor's recommendation, but that isn't what you are doing at all. Your action is not only an expression of what the counselor thinks, but an expression of what you think.

Humility enables our hearts to hear in the middle voice. The ear is the hearing instrument of the body. Humility is the hearing instrument of the spirit. Hearing with the heart is different from hearing with the ear. With the ear we hear once and then live with the memory of having heard. Hearing with the heart means we keep on hearing. It's past tense and present tense at the same time. It's a constant and continual hearing that brings with it the divine enabling (grace) to do and walk in that which we have heard, and still hear, the Father speak or declare. Paul refers to this in Galatians 3:2 when he says, "This is the only thing I want to find out from you: did you receive the Spirit by the works of the Law, or by hearing with faith?"

When we listen with our hearts, we know our identity as Sons and Daughters is anchored in the identity of our Father. We also know the essence of Sonship/Daughterhood means He instructs us so we can abide in His ways and share His life, person, and presence (Ps. 32:8; Heb. 12:7). We are neither the masters of our fate nor do we go about searching for what it is we are supposed to *do*. The Holy Spirit conditions our hearts, and the middle voice is the process by which we "work out our salvation," for it is "God who is at work in us, both to will and to work for His good pleasure." (Phil. 2:13)

At this point in the process of Sonship/Daughterhood, the enemy will try to scuttle what's taking place. In an attempt to derail and distract Jesus, he quoted Scripture (Matt. 4:6). He will do the same with us. His desire is to have us embrace the idea that to please God, the singular focus of our lives must be obedience. If we take the bait, the process of Sonship/Daughterhood will be derailed. The enemy will have neutered us and, rather than living as Sons and Daughters, we will be Laborers, striving on the basis of our own efforts to please a God we would like to get close to, and would like to love, but cannot.

The command given by Jesus is not to obey, but to abide-and-obey. To abide-and-obey (John 15:4) means to remain in the condition of heart wrought by the Holy Spirit through this process of Sonship/Daughterhood Jesus has thus far explained in the beatitudes (Matt. 5:3-14). Trust, dependency, and hearing with the heart are the result. They ensure the focus of our hearts is neither us nor our obedience, which effectively amounts to a self-focus. A singular focus upon obedience keeps our hearts and minds focused upon our own actions. Abiding keeps our hearts and minds stayed upon the Father (Is. 26:3; Col. 3:1,2), which is why abiding is integral to our identity as Sons and Daughters.

A man with the heart identity of a Laborer, for example, identifies with his work, which is where he gets his identity. A man with the heart identity of a Son identifies with his Father, and gets his identity from his Father. To the Laborer, obedience to God flows from himself by an act of his will. To the Son, obedience flows from his heart, and from the reality that his identity is rooted in his Father's identity. The Laborer thinks in terms of achievement and reward. The Son thinks in terms of expression and relationship.

Like Laborers, Sons and Daughters engage in labor, even intense labor, but unlike Laborers, they do not seek or derive identity from it.

Hungering for God

Blessed are those who hunger and thirst for
righteousness, for they shall be satisfied. (Matthew 5:6)

Hunger comes from emptiness, and spiritual emptiness is what the Holy Spirit has revealed and confirmed in us through the first three beatitudes. And now that we are hungering and thirsting for righteousness, the enemy will again attempt to sidetrack us by convincing us that the single focus of our lives must be obedience. The fact that the man or woman walking through this heart-conditioning process has a heightened sensitivity to sin, and a genuine desire to be free of its grasp, makes this deception particularly appealing. But make no mistake—it is a deception. For when our focus is obedience and not hearing and abiding, we take on the heart identity of a Laborer and become estranged from the Father.

An individual with a singular focus upon obedience will not hunger and thirst for righteousness, but hunger and thirst for a clear conscience and a religious life defined by outward form and appearance. People thusly preoccupied will speak affectionately of "commitment," and "passion." This is not to suggest commitment is undesirable or that passion should be shunned, but to recognize that within a healthy relationship, commitment is a consequence, and passion an aroused emotion. Commitment is also a common legal concept. If a man signs a promissory note or contract to provide some type of service or commodity, he makes a commitment. Commitment focuses upon *performance* rather than identity. The term is related to "action" or "delivery."

The Pharisees understood commitment better than anyone else, and used it as a primary grid to measure their value and the value of those around them. Men and women with the heart identity of a Laborer do the same. They think commitment reflects spiritual temperature. Sons and Daughters are different. They know their Father is not interested in the temperature of their commitment but the condition of their heart, for it is from the heart the issues of life flow. (Prov. 4:23)

Even in human endeavors, the richest relationships are not cemented by commitment but love, and in such relationships, commitment is not a cause but a consequence. A husband who truly loves and delights in his wife rarely, if ever, uses the word "commitment" when describing his affection for her. His thoughts will go to her voice, her hair, and the way of her heart. He knows the feel of her hand, the curve of her hip, the tilt of her head, and the look of her eye. In eight chapters and 117 verses, the Old Testament's Song of Solomon doesn't mention commitment. It speaks of a bride who longs to be kissed and a groom who delights in her love. It tells of excited anticipation at the sound of an approaching footstep and the union of lovers. It is for good reason the word commitment is not there. Mature lovers tend not to use it.

If a man truly loves his wife and is asked whether he is committed to her, he will likely have to pause and think about it before he can answer. He will, no doubt, respond in the affirmative, but he'll have to pause and think about it before he answers because he doesn't think of her in those terms. For him, commitment is not the essence of the relationship, but a definable consequence of it.

When love is absent, if a married couple is to stay together then a substitute bonding agent must be found. It's the same for a Christian who walks in self-sufficiency instead of Sonship/Daughterhood. In both of these situations commitment becomes the all-purpose glue. Many relationships are held together by commitment, but the only time it ever becomes a relational focus, or is even talked about very much, is when love is absent, or immature. Mature lovers tend not to think about it, and never part ways in the morning by looking back over their shoulder as they head off to work in order to shout, "I am committed to you!"

This is what the Apostle Paul was talking about when he explained that a person could sacrifice all he possesses, including his life, yet not profit by it (I Cor. 13:3). He is talking about commitment. In the passage, Paul isn't saying we shouldn't help people or be committed to things. He is saying that the real issues of life are of the heart. It means if we condition ourselves, or are conditioned by others, to believe righteousness is nurtured by commitment, we surrender Sonship/Daughterhood. (For many, this is the point at which spiritual identity theft occurs.)

While Laborers seek or derive a kind of self-satisfaction from commitment, and believe it leads to righteousness, Sons and Daughters recognize that hungering for righteousness and hungering for their Father are exactly the same thing. From their hearts they cry with the Psalmist, "My soul thirsts for you," "My soul longs for you" (Ps. 63:1; Ps. 143:6). And they echo the cry of Paul's heart: "that I might know Him and the power of His resurrection!" (Phil. 3:10). Sons and Daughters know that only the presence of their Father will satisfy their hunger, and quench their thirst. They will not rely upon a counterfeit.

The Merciful Heart

Blessed are the merciful,
for they shall receive mercy. (Matthew 5:7)

The first three beatitudes, confessing our poverty of spirit, mourning our condition, and responding in humility, condition our hearts. They empty us. They prepare us. They align our heart so we may know Sonship/Daughterhood. The fourth beatitude, hungering and thirsting for righteousness, is a consequence of the first three. The fifth, showing mercy to those who seemingly do not deserve it, and receiving it ourselves when we don't deserve it, is the Father's way of answering our cry for righteousness.[14]

The predicament we face is that the righteousness for which we long, and that He requires (Matt. 5:48), is not a function of behavior but identity. The "Lord looks upon the heart" (I Sam. 16:7), and no man has the ability to change his heart. The wishing to do so is present, but the ability to change is not (Rom. 7:18). Like the psalmist, we must cry, "Create in me a clean heart, O God." (Ps. 51:10)

As the process of this creation of a new heart unfolds, the nearness of our Father's presence increasingly exposes the deficiencies in our own hearts, making our spiritual need ever more glaring and visible. We are distressed. We seek the Lord's mercy, forgiveness, and cleansing. He answers by reminding us of His ways, that they are higher than our ways (Is. 55:9), and that even as He forgives our sins and extends mercy to the undeserving, He requires that we do the same.

At such a time, extending mercy and forgiveness to those who have hurt us is not in us. Our intuitive sense of justice gives rise to an inner voice that demands a consequence for sin. We know a crime without a consequence is an injustice, be it literal or moral, and if the crime has been committed against us we are especially interested in justice and want to see it satisfied. But our Father, who is "rich in mercy" (Eph. 2:4), knows "mercy triumphs over judgment" (James 2:13), and that having our hearts washed in His mercy will change the essence of who we are.

Extending mercy and forgiving those who have sinned against us confirms we are Sons and Daughters. Jesus said exactly that in Matthew 5:43-45, and makes it clear that it expresses Sonship/Daughterhood: "I say to you, love your enemies and pray for those who persecute you, so that you may be sons of your Father who is in heaven."

Extending and receiving mercy is so integral to our spiritual lives that Jesus included it in the prayer He taught the disciples, which we now call The Lord's Prayer:

> "Forgive us our debts as we also have forgiven our debtors." He added: "If you forgive others for their transgressions, your heavenly Father will also forgive you. But if you do not forgive others, then your Father will not forgive your transgressions." (Matt. 6:12,14,15)

The giving and receiving of mercy is how the Father reshapes our hearts, shares His identity, and confirms our Sonship/Daughterhood. This is not to say we begin overlooking things in people, or that the Father overlooks things in us. On the contrary, as we abide in the condition of grace and the ensuing excavation wrought in our hearts by the Holy Spirit, we are fully aware of the pain, cost, and tragedy of the sins we commit, as well as those committed against us. Nevertheless, the Father calls for us to extend mercy and forgiveness to those who have hurt us, be it a parent or spouse, someone who told lies about us, an unfaithful friend, the thief who stole from us, or an annoying coworker.

The Father's demand that we extend mercy means we receive mercy, but the implication is more far-reaching. As we give and receive mercy, we come to know what our Father is like, and we see ourselves as His Sons and Daughters dependent upon Him for everything we need pertaining to life and godliness. (II Pet. 1:3)

Increasingly acquainted with the extent to which we have been forgiven, and the true nature of His righteous disposition, we grow in our understanding that "he who is forgiven much loves much." (Luke 7:43)

This continual cleansing results in dependency. The absence of self-sufficiency means the ongoing humility in which He enables us to walk brings ever more of the Father's life and fullness to us. He gives grace to the humble. The result is that we become intimately acquainted with the redemptive heart of our Father toward others and ourselves.[15] We begin to see Him as He is, and see others around us as God our Father sees them, no matter how needy or vile. We find our identity in our Father. We are His Sons and Daughters.

Seeing the Father

Blessed are the pure in heart,
for they shall see God. (Matthew 5:8)

The purity of heart Jesus refers to in this sixth beatitude is a consequence of the heart realignment the Holy Spirit has fostered in us through the first five beatitudes. In the fifth, nurtured and led by the Holy Spirit, we experienced what it means to give and receive mercy, which washes and purifies our hearts, making us able to experience what it means to "see" God. When the Bible speaks of seeing God it doesn't mean to see His form in a specific geographic location. The Father dwells in unapproachable light (I Tim. 6:16) and no man can see God and live. (Ex. 33:20)

When the Bible says the "pure in heart shall see God," it refers to the eyes of our hearts. In Matthew 13:15 and again in Acts 28:27, Scripture makes clear that a dull heart and unseeing eye are the same thing. One is figurative of the other. In Ephesians 1:18, Paul affirms this when he makes reference to the eyes of the heart. He petitions the Father on behalf of the Ephesians to have the "eyes of their heart enlightened."

Seeing God means having ears that hear and a heart that is able to receive and abide in that which the Father bestows. It means knowing His thoughts (I Cor. 2:11,12), even as sons and daughters come to know the thoughts of their natural father. Seeing God also means not fleeing obstacles or times of barrenness.

Those who see God, rest in, feed upon, and submit to His faithfulness in the midst of the issues of life (I Cor. 1:9; Ps. 37:3), for they know He makes even the desert to bloom (Is. 51:3), and will perfect that which concerns them (Phil. 1:6; Rom. 8:28). Their identity and dependence is not within themselves or upon themselves, but in their Father.

The inability to see God was the great dilemma of the Israelites after they departed Egypt. They saw His "work for forty years" but went "astray in their heart" (Heb. 3:9,10). They were blind to see that the circumstance in which He placed them was the very avenue through which He intended to bless them. In resisting the circumstance, they resisted God. They either forgot or didn't know that all spiritual life is conceived in the barrenness of an empty womb. Sons and Daughters know their lives are empty, and that if they do bring forth a bounty or blessing, it is because, in the midst of their barrenness, the Father plants within them that which is born of Him.

Re-presenting Christ[16]

Blessed are the peacemakers,
for they shall be called sons of God. (Matthew 5:9)

We are now coming to the practical implications of Sonship/Daughterhood. We have experienced the Father's ways, but we also know and see His heart and disposition toward the people and circumstances around us—our church, city, family, friends, and coworkers, including people who have sinned against us. Because our identity is rooted in Him, we are fully dependent upon Him. We share His life and disposition. (John 15:3-9)

From the heart, we now understand that when the Bible says the Father has given us eternal life (John 3:15; I John 5:13), it isn't referring to living our own lives in a linear sense, that is to say, a duration of time without end. Rather, it means knowing the Father and having Him share His life with us, which is much more than longevity (Eph. 1:3-12). Eternal life is the Father's life and to know Him is to know life.

> "And this is eternal life, that they may know You, the only true God, and Jesus Christ whom You have sent."
> (John 17:3)

Now that we have come to possess in humility the disposition of our Father toward others, we do things without grumbling or disputing because we are quite literally "children of God above reproach in the midst of a crooked and perverse generation, among whom [we] appear as lights in the world" (Phil. 2:15) and to whom we are ambassadors. (II Cor. 5:17)

An ambassador is the literal and personified expression of a nation or kingdom. For example, when the U.S. ambassador to Saudi Arabia presents himself to that country's head of state, for all practical purposes, the ambassador *is* the United States. When he speaks, the United States speaks. When he signs a trade document or diplomatic agreement, the United States signs. Within the Kingdom of Saudi Arabia, the presence of the U.S. ambassador is the presence of the United States.

So it is with our Father's kingdom. Being a peacemaker means we are the emissaries Paul writes of in II Corinthians 5:17, when he states we are ambassadors of Christ and His kingdom. In John 18:36,37, Jesus assures Pilate He is a king, and that His kingdom is not of this world. Indeed, He is the Prince of Peace (Is. 9:6), and His kingdom is an everlasting kingdom of righteousness and peace. (Rom. 14:17)

As Sons and Daughters of the Eternal Father, we are the personification of His kingdom on earth (I John 3:2; Heb. 12:7; Eph. 1:5; Rom. 8:15; Gal. 4:6). The Father's Spirit literally dwells within us (Rom. 8:10), which means we know His thoughts (I Cor. 2:11-13). As Sons and Daughters, we quite literally have the mind of Christ (I Cor. 2:16). We are peacemakers because the Prince of Peace is within us. (II Cor. 13:5)

Author and pastor Francis Frangipane says at this point in the process of holiness, a believer quite literally becomes a New Testament prophet. Indeed, in Matthew 5:12, Jesus compares men and women who have walked through this process of Sonship/Daughterhood with prophets who have gone before.

They are not Old Testament prophets who pronounce judgment, but New Testament prophets who "re"-present (as in *again* present) the person of Christ.[17]

Peacemakers offer themselves to God, desiring that the Father's ways, heart, and mercy be known in the lives of others. Because they feed on the mercy and faithfulness of their Father, instead of judging others, they bring peace to them by praying for them and blessing them. Peacemakers know the Father doesn't want to condemn sinners (John 3:17) or struggling saints (Is. 42:3), but desires to redeem them and bless them. To do so, He uses Sons and Daughters whose hearts have been aligned, conditioned, and shaped by His grace, wisdom, and righteousness. We are peacemakers in the sense that our lives are a literal peace offering.[18]

We willingly give ourselves for the rescue and blessing of others, even as Jesus did, with a view to the redemption that will follow.

You Will Be Accused...

Blessed are those who have been persecuted for the
sake of righteousness, for theirs is the kingdom of heaven.
(Matthew 5:10)

It is at this point in the process that we are the greatest threat to the enemy, and this is why we will be persecuted, insulted, and falsely accused. More than once, the enemy has sought to sidetrack us by turning us into Laborers who are focused on our own obedience and legalism. In response to the Spirit, we have humbled ourselves. As a result, we have come to know Sonship/Daughterhood more fully, and the joy when obedience to the Father flows from our identity in Him rather than the mind and will of a Laborer. In practice and in reality the source of our identity is not ourselves, our own obedience or efforts, but the identity of our Father. By the work of His hands, by His Spirit, He has wrought in our hearts a literal "re"-presentation[19] of the person of Christ and His kingdom. "It is no longer I who live but Christ lives in me." (Gal. 2:20)

To discredit or marginalize what the Father has wrought, the enemy will accuse us, even working through other Christians who do not have the heart identity of Sons and Daughters. Accusations will be based on past sins, mistakes, or false assumptions about the way Christians are supposed to be—ideas rooted in paradigms other than that of a Son/Daughter. The words we speak will be taken out of context and used to accuse us. To the degree we expect to be fairly dealt with in life and circumstance, and resent this unfair treatment, we will be hindered, perhaps even crippled. Men and women sometimes miss out on the provisions of Sonship/Daughterhood due to such attacks. They do not realize that what the enemy could not do through the entire process of learning to walk as a Son or Daughter, he succeeded in doing by accusations and our own expectation of fair treatment by others.

You Are the Salt of the Earth;
You Are the Light of the World.
(Matthew 5:13,14)

In these two verses, Jesus is not telling us what to do, but confirming what has already taken place within us. We are the salt of the earth and light of the world not because of our achievement or effort, but because of what the Father has wrought in our hearts and minds through this process of Sonship/Daughterhood.

Through the darkness of our spiritual poverty and need, the identity of our Father shines:

"For God, who said, 'Light shall shine out of darkness,' is the One who has shone in our hearts to give the Light of the knowledge of the glory of God." (II Cor. 4:6)

	LABORER	ORPHAN	BEGGAR	SON/DAUGHTER
CONCEPT OF GOD	Strict, demanding, showing favor only to those who earn it and please Him.	Compares what they have known from the past regarding a father figure with what they hope He might be like.	The ultimate controller; One who is distant; One to be afraid of.	Father, Daddy / Abba (Gal. 4:6).
SOURCE OF IDENTITY	Self-sufficiency, work, achievement, position or status, the expectation of future reward or payment for services rendered.	Persistent need, being comfortless, awareness that Sonship/Daughterhood is missing, inability to see how it might be procured.	Being a victim, unforgiveness, sense of being a whole person is corrupted or has been stolen.	An extension of the identity of their Father. They engage in labor (even intense labor) but do not find identity in it.
MOTIVE FOR OBEDIENCE	To please God, obtain recognition, and/or receive a reward.	Fear of being rejected, the desire for acceptance and approval.	Obey with willingness only when the consequence not to becomes so painful they see no option.	Identify with their Father and hear His voice (John 10:4), obedience is an expression of identity and love (John 14:15).

	LABORER	ORPHAN	BEGGAR	SON/DAUGHTER
RESPONSE TO SPIRITUAL BARRENNESS	Fear barrenness, flee it, view it as weakness that needs to be overcome by increased busyness.	Respond to barrenness by withdrawing or seeking a surrogate father/son or father/daughter relationship.	Unaware of barrenness.	Respond to barrenness by declaring, "I have need" (Matt. 5:3), rather than fleeing it, they submit it to their Father, affirming their dependence on Him.
BIBLICAL EXAMPLE	Older brother in the Parable of the Prodigal (Luke 15).	The prodigal prior to his experience in Luke 15:17, when he "came to himself" (KJV).	The lame man in John 5, King Ahab (I Kings 21).	John (I John 3), Jesus, the prodigal son after he "came to himself" (Luke 15:17 KJV).
FUTURE HOPE/FUTURE EXPECTATION	To be rewarded, then abide in their earned status.	The hope of being approved of and accepted by a father figure.	God's vengeance on villains.	More of their Father Himself; walking in righteousness, peace and joy (John 10:10).

Chart Notes

The heart identities presented in the chart on the previous two pages are characteristic of born-again believers. However, there are other heart identities that shape the lives of non-believers. One example is the heart identity of a Moralist.

A Moralist is a man or woman whose heart's response to truth is pride and self-sufficiency. Moralists live in a values-driven paradigm with themselves at the center, rather than God. Unlike Christian legalists, who are also values-driven but often appear controlling or fearful, Moralists appear calm, seemingly serene. This is because Moralists deny the authority and existence of God. Consciously or unconsciously, they believe they are God, or at the very least, have the capacity to become like God. (Gen. 3:5)

A values-driven legalist (Laborer) knows he is not God and that he is therefore accountable to the Almighty. Moralists believe there is no accountability or consequence for sin, apart from the impact it has on immediate physical conditions, their own conscience, and the delaying effect on their journey to be *like God.* They find identity in the *moral journey* or *life journey* they are on, and what they believe to be a never-ending character improvement process. They may or may not acknowledge a spirit world. But unlike Paul, who wrote, "there is none righteous, not even one" (Rom. 3:10), Moralists believe all people are basically good and have the ability not only to act righteously, but to *be* righteous.

Part Seven

Motivational Gifts: Their

Purpose & Characteristics

Expressing Heart Identity

Only after we understand our identity as Sons and Daughters can we comprehend the God-intended function of motivational gifts. Described by the Apostle Paul in Romans 12:6-8, motivational gifts are divine endowments. They are inclinations or intuitive abilities that the Father has woven into the disposition of every person.

> We have gifts that differ according to the grace given to us: prophecy, in proportion to faith; ministry, in ministering; the teacher, in teaching; the exhorter, in exhortation; the giver, in generosity; the leader[20], in diligence; the compassionate, in cheerfulness. (Rom. 12:6-8 NRSV)

These divine endowments the Father has given are as much a part of us as our DNA. We go to bed with our gifts, wake up with them, and take them to work in the morning. They're there when we attend family reunions, play a round of golf, eat dinner, or sing in the shower. They're a more integral part of our person than our arms, legs, or eyes. We can lose an arm or an eye and still be a living person, but we cannot lose our motivational gifts any more than we can change our blood type. In brief, the motivational gifts are:

Perception—(Prophecy) An intuitive capacity to discern and accurately read situations.
Serving—(Ministry) The heartfelt desire to meet the practical needs of others.

Teaching—(Researching) The motivation to find clarity through study and research.

Exhortation—The innate desire to encourage others to grow and develop, even in the face of hardship and suffering.

Giving—The inborn desire to contribute generously of financial and other resources.

Administration—The desire to coordinate people, resources, and schedules.

Compassion—The capacity to identify with, and the desire to comfort, those in distress.

Each of us has a unique mixture of gifts, though one of them tends to dominate and influence the way we see and respond to situations and establish priorities. If we walk with the heart identity of Sons/Daughters, our hearts will be open to the prompting of the Holy Spirit, and our giftedness will be a practical extension of what the Father is working in us. We will minister with the grace He gives in the way He indicates we should. The focus will not be the gift, but the Father.

If we do not have the heart identity of Sons/Daughters, our focus will be on our own fulfillment and what we can do with our gift. It is an erroneous disposition that has led more than a few people to falsely conclude that their gift and their identity are synonymous.

Gifts exercised apart from a hearing heart can actually oppose the purposes of God. In fact, much of what we call spiritual warfare is simply God resisting our efforts to use our gifts to build or achieve something that He never called us to. God resists the proud and self-determined. (I Peter 5:5)

Humility is the prerequisite to Sonship/Daughterhood, a hearing heart, and the mature functioning of the gifts.

For example, a person with a gift of giving who is not walking in Sonship and hearing with his heart has unwittingly made himself vulnerable. Though his internal motivation is to give, he does not hear the Father's prompting, and will therefore be subject to manipulation by emotional pleas or promises, even personal ambition. Needs that the Father wants to meet will go unmet, and the giver's resources will be used in ways the Father did not intend. Similarly, a person with a compassion gift who is not walking in Sonship/Daughterhood may try to rescue someone out of a particular circumstance that God has ordained for the specific purpose of shaping that person into His image.

Understanding the proper role and function of the Romans 12 gifts becomes even more critical in church structures headed by leaders with the heart identity of Laborers. A leader who finds his identity in his achievements, and what he constructs, views people as resources or commodities to accomplish an agenda, and their motivational gifts as levers of power to employ. This is why gift teaching in congregations led by Laborers is usually used to recruit people to perform the tasks of the institution and to participate in its programs. Gift discovery programs are even called by titles like "Discover Your Gifts and Help Your Church Grow." Those who have the gifts of compassion, serving, or giving are usually thought to be the most useful.

Those who do not have the gifts of compassion, serving, or giving may sometimes find themselves on the fringe of the institution, often without understanding why. A man with a perception gift, for example, will find it difficult to stay in an institutional church led by Laborers, especially if he has the heart identity of a Son. Though he will intuitively see wrong motivations, he will not have the freedom to express what he senses, and if he comments on it, he will likely be viewed as unsupportive or rebellious. Often, for the sake of "unity," the Laborer-leader will attempt to sideline the perceiver or get rid of him entirely. When this occurs, the resulting wounds in the one with the perception gift are doubly painful because they were inflicted by someone who should have been nurturing and trustworthy. In truth, as we will see in Parts Eight and Nine, it can be dangerous to the spiritual life of those with the gift of perception to be in an institution led by a leader with the heart identity of a Laborer.

Laborers often fail to recognize that each of us is unique and that God has made each of us for a different function. For example, Laborers who have the gift of giving and are motivated to meet the material needs of others will assume that everyone is just like them. If they have the gift of perception, they assume everyone can see what they see. When others do not give, or see as they expect them to, they assume it is because people are indifferent or uncooperative. Laborers do not understand the diversity of the grace that God has given to each of us.

Value of Knowing and Understanding Motivational Gifts:

- Enables us to recognize a God-ordained place to express our giftedness in the midst of our relationships and circumstances. (I Cor. 3:9)
- Makes us better able to understand our feelings and responses.

- Makes us better able to understand the feelings and responses of others.

- Provides parents with a better understanding of their children, enabling them to realize that the child's gifts may differ from theirs, and knowing this, to be discerning of their actions and choices as they discipline, guide, and teach.

- Fosters cooperation as we understand that the gifts complement one another, and that the gifts others have are diverse, needed, and valuable.

- Enables us to interact with others in more appropriate, specific, and meaningful ways.

The Perceiver Gift
"Discernment-oriented"

Definition: The sensor—intuitively sees beyond the obvious and is motivated to assess or comment upon the implications of actions and decisions.

Body Part: Eyes.

Need Met: Directional.

Characteristics of those with the perception gift:
- Are the eyes of the body; see what others often cannot see.
- Ability to see makes them a valuable source of perspective and direction.
- May find themselves alone or misunderstood because others cannot see what they see.
- Often find themselves standing against the crowd.
- Intuitively discern character and motives.
- Reject dishonesty, including hypocrisy and manipulation.
- Tend to speak frankly, declaring what they see regardless of the consequence.
- Have a strong dependence on Scripture to validate their convictions.
- Often called to intercession because of the insight they have.

Potential manifestations when maturity is absent or the heart identity is other than that of a Son/Daughter:
- Want to fix people and situations rather than pray.
- May be judgmental.
- May overlook the need and role of the administration gift to bring vision to reality.
- May be more concerned with rightness than relationships.

- May lack sensitivity for the feelings of others.
- Can be too forceful and intimidate others by their frankness.
- Can be too cut and dried and even inflexible when working with others.
- May find intimate personal relationships hindered by frankness and strict standards—the result being a lonely person who feels rejected.
- May slip into a negative attitude, becoming cynical or pessimistic.
- Often misunderstood and criticized—markedly greater potential for rebellion if they fail to abide in the Father's provision of Sonship/Daughterhood.

To mature if you have the perception gift:
- Walk in humility; God is opposed to the proud but gives grace to the humble.
- Listen to others and temper your words with love.
- Practice patience and tenderness so your voice can be heard with social grace and love rather than harsh words or abruptness.
- Learn to cast your cares upon the Lord and abide in Him and His provision to find release from the burden of knowledge about difficult situations or wrong motives.

Biblical example:
Peter (Acts 5); John the Baptist (John 7:18-20).

The Serving Gift
"Oriented to serve"

Definition: The worker, motivated to meet practical needs.
Body Part: Hands.
Need Met: Practical.

Characteristics of those with the serving gift:
- Great desire to help with practical needs, volunteering even for menial tasks.
- React quickly to needs, not wanting to deal with red tape; often work alone.
- Quiet, don't speak a lot, cooperative, supportive; shun a high profile.
- Willing to spend long hours to get the job done.
- Most often behind the scenes, frequently doing jobs to free others to carry out their gifting.
- Express love by doing something for a person; prefer to give gifts they have made.
- Prefer short-range goals to long-range goals.
- Bored with planning and procedures that talk about what needs to be done.

Potential manifestations when maturity is absent or the heart identity is other than that of a Son/Daughter:
- May experience woundedness if they don't feel appreciated.
- Find it difficult to say no.
- Often suffer from exhaustion or exploitation by others.
- May conclude they are inadequate or unqualified for leadership roles, including those in marriage and the home.

- Can become critical of others who are unwilling to pitch in or not as willing as they are.
- May have difficulty being served by others.
- Eagerness to serve may be misjudged as ambition.

To mature if you have the serving gift:
- Walk in humility; God is opposed to the proud but gives grace to the humble.
- Be aware of the tendency to be critical of others who do not share your serving attitude.
- Learn to say no.
- Deliberately recognize and honor those whose gifts are different from yours.
- Remember that not all needs are physical.
- Be reminded that by God's design, servers tend not to see the big picture—learn to have appropriate regard for existing protocols and procedures.

Biblical example:
Martha (Luke 10:38-40); John Mark (II Timothy 4:11).

The Teaching Gift
"Learning-oriented"

Definition: The analyzer—motivated to know details and systematize findings.

Body Part: Mind.

Need Met: Intellectual.

Characteristics of those with the teaching gift:
- Like to gather as many facts as they can about a problem or subject, explaining why men and women with a teaching gift make good researchers.
- Oriented to present their findings, research, or knowledge in a systematic way.
- Concerned with accuracy of words; alert to factual details that may go unnoticed by others.
- Enjoy the world of books and ideas.
- Organize facts so people can reach conclusions and make intelligent decisions.
- Systematize learning so enlightened understanding is effectively passed on to others.
- Insist on validating facts and knowing the authority source of new concepts.

Potential manifestations when maturity is absent or the heart identity is other than that of a Son/Daughter:
- May become more interested in factual detail than practical application.
- May unduly emphasize details, boring or frustrating listeners.

- May enjoy research more than involvement with people; may become loners, living in a self-contained world.
- May be dogmatic and legalistic.
- May become proud of their knowledge and learning.
- May procrastinate in decision-making, believing more information might be available to influence their decision.
- May become critical when they spot even slight factual errors in things taught by others.
- May convey a lack of warmth or feeling because of their inordinate desire to appear objective.

To mature if you have the teaching gift:

- Walk in humility; God is opposed to the proud but gives grace to the humble.
- Remember that disseminating facts is important, but change is of the heart.
- Be reminded that position and accomplishment may open doors for you, but God is not a respecter of persons. He has regard for the lowly (Ps. 138:6).
- Equip yourself with the tools of effective communication, for "the tongue of the wise brings healing" (Prov. 12:18), and "makes knowledge acceptable" (Prov. 15:2).

Biblical example:

Luke the "beloved physician" (Luke 1:1-4). This passage contains the biblical definition of a teacher. The Book of Acts, also penned by Luke, gives evidence of his attention to learning and detail.

The Exhortation Gift
"Message-oriented"

Definition: The encourager—motivated to build people up.
Body Part: Mouth.
Need Met: Motivational.

Characteristics of those with the exhortation gift:
- Love to talk; positive, upbeat, and adaptable.
- Believe people can learn from every problem.
- See potential in people; counsel and encourage them to overcome the past.
- Act as advocates.
- Act as a counselor or motivator.
- Aim for the heart rather than the mind.
- Love to teach the practical application of truth.
- Love to give specific and practical prescriptions to overcome problems.
- See suffering and hardship as avenues for growth and maturity.

Potential manifestations when maturity is absent or the heart identity is other than that of a Son/Daughter:
- Can have a tendency to interrupt others in their eagerness to give their opinion or advice.
- May be manipulative, especially when they have the heart identity of a Laborer.
- To support their position they may use reference material, including Bible verses, out of context.
- May be outspoken, opinionated, and come across with overly simplistic solutions.

• Feed on their capacity to effect change; can become impatient when working with people who do not show quick improvement.

To mature if you have the exhortation gift:
• Walk in humility; God is opposed to the proud but gives grace to the humble.
• Deliberately and consciously ask the Holy Spirit to help you analyze any motivational and positive-thinking philosophies, self-help books, or how-to manuals you might read in light of God's word.
• Recognize and be reminded that all people have genuine limitations in accordance with their maturity and gifting.

Biblical example:
Paul (Colossians 1:28-29).

The Giving Gift
"Cause-oriented"

Definition: The support raiser—motivated to gather resources, as well as to use personal resources to support worthwhile projects.

Body Part: Arms (Extend the reach of what they give to).

Need Met: Material.

Characteristics of those with the giving gift:
- Desire to connect resources with needs, even when they aren't providing the actual resources.
- Greatest joy is being an answer to someone's prayer.
- Do not limit their giving to money.
- Often give anonymously to worthwhile projects.
- Give financially, but also participate in the ministry or project.
- Motivate others to give and organize fundraising for special needs.
- Generally, have an aversion to stewardship campaigns or slick programs to raise funds.
- Have the ability to discern wise purchases and investments; save to give away.
- Are intuitively business-minded.

Potential manifestations when maturity is absent or the heart identity is other than that of a Son/Daughter:
- Can become cause-oriented rather than people-oriented.
- May be judgmental toward people who are poor financial managers.

119

- May attempt to gain control through their giving.
- May give without consent of spouse, leading to hurt feelings and relational conflict in the home.

To mature if you have the giving gift:
- Walk in humility; God is opposed to the proud but gives grace to the humble.
- Recognize you have a *seeing* gift with regard to finances and that God will give you patience and compassion for those with financial management difficulties.
- Be reminded that being successful involves more than money.
- Beware of linking your giving with a desire for recognition (Matt. 6:1-4).

Biblical example:
Abraham (Genesis 13:1-11, 24:1,34-35); Dorcas (Acts 9:36-39).

The Administration Gift
"Process-oriented"

Definition: The organizer—motivated to consider and evaluate available resources and apply them into a functioning unit or system, even if that system is simply a mother's routine to get her children prepared and off to school.

Body Part: Shoulders.

Need Met: Functional.

Characteristics of those with the administration gift:
- Intuitively understand the necessary steps to achieve established priorities.
- Have the ability to coordinate resources to achieve priorities.
- Able to delegate; know what can and cannot be delegated and to whom.
- Hold people accountable for their particular area of responsibility.
- Have an unusual ability to withstand criticism/opposition.
- Within the context of an administrative project, have the ability to place people into areas where they can help bring about the desired result.
- Are self-starters; diligent and not easily sidetracked.
- Assume responsibility and are willing to personally sacrifice to accomplish operational goals.

Potential manifestations when maturity is absent or the heart identity is other than that of a Son/Daughter:
- Trust and rely upon systems or processes.
- Can inadvertently conclude criticism of the system is criticism of them, especially if they designed or built it.

- Inclined to be task-oriented rather than people-oriented.
- If not careful, will use people to achieve their agenda, over-using or burning out those who are loyal, faithful, and willing to work.
- When set in a senior position of institutional authority, can become controllers, believing control is the means to bring about the desired end.
- May develop an outer callousness due to being a target for criticism.
- Due to their confidence in planning and related systems, may have a tendency not to listen to the observations and advice of others.
- Can fail to recognize that the administration gift is related to a management or operational function rather than long-term overall direction.
- Can mistake authority that flows from an office or title with a personal mantle of leadership.

To mature if you have the administration gift:
- Walk in humility; God is opposed to the proud but gives grace to the humble.
- Remember that other people, particularly perceivers, will see things you cannot—administration is just one gift of many, and biblical authority structures are not pyramidical (Mark 10:42,43; Matt. 20:25-28).
- Learn to communicate to others the valuable nature of their contribution.

Biblical example:
Nehemiah (Nehemiah 2:5-8); Joseph (Genesis 37-50); The Virtuous Woman (Proverbs 31).

The Compassion Gift
"People-oriented"

Definition: The feeler—motivated to meet the emotional needs of others.

Body Part: Heart.

Need Met: Emotional—The compassion gift is able to meet a need that is deeper than emotional woundedness. People with this gift, anointed by the Holy Spirit, are able to touch the deepest part of a sufferer's being, convey the Father's disposition and grace, and as a consequence, bring healing. Emotional needs are met, but the healing and ministry that takes place occur at a deeper level than emotions alone.

Characteristics of those with the compassion gift:
- Motivated to take action to relieve suffering.
- Quick to identify with the emotional pain of others.
- Tendency to operate by how they feel more than on facts.
- Believe the best in everyone.
- Generally avoid actions that hurt the feelings of others.
- Reveal the nature of God by showing unconditional acceptance, kindness, and care to hurting people.
- Have a strong desire to see all conflicts cease and people unified.
- Willing to spend time with people in need, to listen or provide a shoulder to cry on.

Potential manifestations when maturity is absent or the heart identity is other than that of a Son/Daughter:
- In group settings, may avoid making a decision if it is not by consensus.

- Have difficulty being on time; don't plan ahead.
- May compromise because they consider not hurting another person's feelings more important than truth.
- May become so emotionally involved they lose objectivity.
- Propensity to establish emotional connections may inadvertently lead to improper involvement with the opposite sex.
- May become closed in spirit to insensitive or insincere people.
- Tendency to avoid "speaking the truth in love" can lead to diminished effectiveness, including parental discipline toward children.
- May repress healthy negative feelings, then lash out when the pressure is too great.
- May become susceptible to depression and even a root of bitterness because of their close identification with the emotional pain of others.
- If not abiding in prayer and walking in the provision God makes available, may become vulnerable to addictions to sooth pain.
- Eagerness to help may be misjudged as a desire to get involved in other people's business.

To mature if you have the compassion gift:
- Walk in humility; God is opposed to the proud but gives grace to the humble.
- Learn to speak the truth in love.
- Recognize God allows and even ordains suffering and struggles in order to give people an opportunity to abandon their self-sufficiency.
- Recognize you cannot be a rescuer in every situation.

• Be constantly reminded that feelings are not necessarily a reliable or accurate measurement of truth.

Biblical example:

Good Samaritan (Luke 10:30-35); Apostle John (I John, II John, III John).

Part Eight

Implications on Leadership

Laborers as Leaders

The practical consequences of the heart identities and motivational gifts are visible in all areas of our lives, but for the purposes of this chapter, we will look more closely at their impact upon church and church leaders.

Within much of modern society, the dominant culture is that of a Laborer. People readily associate the identity of others with their particular achievements. Ambitious people who effect change are prized—whether that change occurs in politics, economics, popular culture, or even in the church.

Modern society is infatuated with leadership. Leaders are thought to be like automobiles—utilitarian devices able to transport us from one state of being to another. In a Laborer culture, leaders are expected to possess know-how and pass it on to their followers. They are also expected to articulate vision—to paint pictures with words that inspire us, showing us the next step on the road to some type of promised land. But Christians may need to be reminded that vision is not a moral virtue or indication of righteousness.

Just because a leader speaks of vision doesn't necessarily mean his vision is born of God, even if he is the leader of a church. There are artists, business leaders, politicians, and even pornographers with vision.

Due to the constraints of size and context, in this volume we are unable to fully address the way heart identity is manifested in leaders and leadership structures. We will do so in an upcoming volume. However, to provide context as we consider the practical implications of heart identity, in Part Eight we have briefly addressed the way Laborer-leaders manifest heart identity. In Part Ten, we look briefly at the way Son/Daughter-leaders manifest heart identity.

Vladimir Lenin was a visionary. He envisioned a workers' state that would centralize political authority and ensure that a central government owned and controlled the entire means of economic production and distribution. The creation of the Soviet Union was the result—a communist empire with a government that murdered vast numbers of its own citizens. Michael Dell's vision was to provide modestly priced computers to American consumers on a massive scale. Dell Computer Corporation, a giant distributor of personal computers, was the outcome. Bill Clinton's vision was to become president of the United States. Hugh Hefner's vision was to establish a sexually explicit glossy magazine that would redefine cultural morality and make him rich.

Vision, like wisdom, has more than one source. James points out that one kind of wisdom comes from God and that another comes from the heart of man (James 3:13-18). One has fruit that remains; the other does not.

In his gospel, John declares that some things are born of God while other things are born of the will of man or the will of the flesh (John 1:13). It means that one kind of vision is entirely carnal. Another kind of vision is steeped in self-effort and rooted in the human will. A third kind of vision is born of God and deposited in us by the Holy Spirit.[21]

What then should we say about a man or woman who is *doing a work for God*? Bible teacher Ian Thomas,[22] in a wonderful presentation made at Exchanged Life Ministries, says the minute you meet a man who is "doing a work for God, the first thing you know about him is that he is a rebel." He might be a man of vision who inspires with words. He may even have presided over the

129

development and expansion of what is thought to be a successful Christian ministry, or multiple successful Christian ministries. But even so, his seeming success doesn't change the truth of what he is. He is an individual who rejects the eternal truth found in Zechariah 4:6:

> "'Not by might, nor by power, but by my Spirit,' says the Lord of Hosts."

The word translated "power" in this passage is translated elsewhere in Scripture as "force," "strength," "wealth," "fruits," and "substance." In a figurative sense, it means the "capacity to produce," which is the disposition and objective of a man or woman with the heart identity of a Laborer. Unlike Jesus, who did nothing by his own initiative (John 8:28), leaders with a Laborer disposition rely entirely on initiative. They anticipate what future success should look like, not realizing that what they are anticipating actually stems from their own concept of achievement, which is rooted in ambition. Because of their heart attitude and paradigm, they inevitably fall into the trap of mistaking their sincere and heartfelt imaginings for God-given vision.

Two examples of this kind of mis-sourced vision are Daniel and Harold. Both are middle-aged men who have pastored for several years.[23]

Daniel is a highly methodical man. He is also extremely determined. In high school and college, he enjoyed outstanding success in sports, not because he possessed any unusual degree of physical ability, but because he was incredibly tenacious. No matter how daunting, painful, or demanding a task, he simply refused to quit, complain, or give up.

After becoming a believer, through a series of events he could never have predicted, Daniel assumed the pastorate of a congregation with a Sunday attendance of about 250. From the first day, he had ambitions for the church and what he believed his ministry to be. He wanted to love God, and like all Laborers, believed pleasing Him through his labor was the way to do it. He stressed the indispensable role of commitment, spoke regularly about "taking the city for God," and believed "growing the church" (by which he meant his congregation), was how God's kingdom on earth would be expanded. Since he assumed the pastorate, Sunday attendance at Daniel's congregation has grown to nearly 1,200. The number of people on staff has grown, the budget has expanded, and the congregation has moved into a new and much larger building. Several short-term missionary teams were recently sent to Asia. Virtually every night of the week there is a programmed event taking place at the church building.

Since his singular passion is to please God through his labor, Daniel's objective is to teach everyone in the congregation to be a busy and effective Laborer, just like him. And although he has preached sermons to the contrary, the unspoken basis of his heart attitude and paradigm rejects the idea of the church as a body with Christ as the head. Instead, he believes every church operates with the senior pastor as CEO and Christ as a reigning monarch. His manner and teaching style reinforce the notion that the clergy performs the *real* work of the ministry, while the laity goes out into the world, earns a living, and tithes to support the institution, its staff, and its programs.

Daniel sees elders and board members as individuals whose role is to support the pastor and, to that end, he has attracted a group of men around him who share this perspective. He assumes members of the congregation, if spiritually healthy, will want to support him and this small group of leaders. Daniel sees people and their gifts as resources, and the construction, expansion, and maintenance of the institution as his "ministry."

Having the heart identity of a Laborer, Daniel is unable to appreciate the distinction between vision that is born of God and vision that is born of his own heartfelt desire to please God and earn His favor (John 1:13). His belief that he can please God by building a successful institutional church has turned him into a controller. The process is subtle rather than overt, and Daniel is an understated rather than obvious controller. Yet, regardless of the speed with which a person heads his automobile in a particular direction—north, south, east or west—he is still headed in that direction and at some point will arrive at his destination.

Two counties over from Daniel is Pastor Harold. Harold's heart identity of a Laborer is the same as Daniel's, but he lacks Daniel's charisma. While Daniel has an exhortation gift, Harold's primary motivational gift is administration.

Harold is the senior pastor at a congregation in a medium-sized city. There were about 1,400 people attending when he took over. He moved slowly, but in fairly short order, replaced every board member he believed would not support him. He hired a new executive pastor, and ensured the other seven pastors on staff were supportive of his style and approach.

Harold desperately wants his church to grow and influence his city and denomination. He diligently applies every innovative management practice he can lay his hands on. He reads every new book on the subject of church growth, church management, and how to present a user-friendly face to the community. He travels many thousands of miles attending seminars and conferences. He keeps his eyes open for especially capable people he might be able to hire. He uses professional consultants to launch and maintain fundraising programs.

Despite the fact that Harold is using every persuasive technique he can get his hands on, things are not going well. Two years ago, the church split over a doctrinal dispute, and since then has found it increasingly difficult to meet budgetary requirements. The building is in serious need of repair. To compensate for the loss of income, several members of the staff have had to be let go. With the problems have come a host of complainers, each one sure he holds the formula that will restore the congregation to its former glory.

Harold is on a treadmill that is sapping his strength and robbing him of life and peace. His health is failing. He feels pressure on his marriage. His relationship with his two sons is strained. He doesn't like Christians anymore. They're too demanding. He hates being a pastor. He feels like he's in prison. He is burning himself out and he knows it, but in the depths of his Laborer heart, he has come to the conclusion that burnout is simply part of the cost he must pay to serve God and earn His favor.

Almost a year ago, Harold was so exhausted a breakdown seemed imminent. Though he took a six-month sabbatical along the Florida coast to help him deal with the pressure, the source of his stress remains unaddressed. What Harold doesn't know is that his sense of being overwhelmed has nothing to do with how well he has or hasn't done things. Its source is the paradigm through which he sees himself, the church, its activities, its structure, and his own responsibility. It is a paradigm that ensures his congregation's corporate structure is almost entirely dependent upon him. The paradigm of a Laborer has literally brought Harold to the point of despair, and the more faithful and diligent he tries to be in adhering to its demands, the more desperate his life becomes.

Two pastors, Daniel and Harold, both are unable to distinguish between God-given vision that is born and sustained in a dependent heart (Sonship/Daughterhood), and their own desire to construct something from which they derive identity and a sense of success—a desire born and sustained by the will of man (Laborer).

Daniel is considered a successful pastor. Harold is not. Unfortunately, they are both missing the mark, not because of the results they generate or fail to generate, but because of the paradigm in which they operate. Their belief that God is well pleased by the deliberate application of know-how to build institutional structures is not the scriptural basis of Christian ministry or of the church. "Not by might nor by power but by My Spirit," says the Lord of Hosts. (Zech. 4:6)

Unfortunately, people graduating from academic institutions and entering Christian service are seldom taught to consider the subtle but real distinction between heartfelt ambition and God-given vision, and the different types of institutional structures and cultures that emerge from them. Consequently, a good number of pastors and church leaders begin on the basis of what God has genuinely put in their hearts; yet, because of the expectations foisted upon them by the religious system (or their own Laborer heart identity), they end up living in a circumstance they didn't anticipate—wearing a mantle they didn't expect. They take on the responsibilities of CEOs within institutional structures that effectively practice central planning—a leadership model in which decision-making is highly centralized and controlled. This centralized approach to church leadership, combined with the belief that most people are laity while only a few are clergy, results in clear expectations of what a pastor or church leader is supposed to do and be. The unspoken assumption is that the way a pastor proves his mettle and pleases God is by generating specific results.

Daniel and Harold are not unique. Many church leaders are in the same position. They labor, sacrifice, and in many instances burn themselves out. When we mistake ambition for vision and accomplishment for the fruit of abiding Sonship/Daughterhood, no matter how sincere or well-meaning our intent, we are Laborers, estranged from the Father. We become the elder brother in Luke's parable of the prodigal who labored for his father (Luke 15:11), lived in the same house as his father, but never knew his father's heart or enjoyed extended times of easy rest in his presence.

A Hearing Heart or Personal Initiative

Many Christians speak affectionately of men and women who "achieved great things for God"—people like George Mueller, Gladys Aylward, Hudson Taylor, John Hyde, and Corrie ten Boom influential people who brought about change. Some biographers mistakenly refer to these individuals as spiritual giants. In truth, they were nothing of the kind. They were men and women whose so-called great achievements came about only because they had the heart identity of Sons and Daughters. Their lives were visible expressions of an internal reality born of God and unfolded by grace. They lived in a state of dependency. As a result, they surrendered their barrenness to the work of the Holy Spirit, and came to understand the profound truth embodied in the phrase:

"It is normal for a father to ask his son (or daughter) to help him do things."

Jesus Himself knew the truth of this statement. He affirmed it in John 8:28, when He said, "I do nothing on my own initiative." In speaking of this passage, Bible teacher James Stone asks, "When Jesus said He did 'nothing' on his own initiative did He mean what He said? Does nothing mean nothing?"[24] Good question. The dictionary says nothing means "not anything, nonexistence, zero, not at all." Initiative means "originating new ideas or methods."

In a presentation made at Exchanged Life Ministries, Bible teacher Ian Thomas[25] eloquently makes the same point:

Never imagine that when you look at the Lord Jesus as [a] man on earth that you are looking simply at a superman— let alone a superstar. You are just looking at [a] man.... Everything [Jesus] did, the Father was the one doing it. Everything He said, the Father was the one saying it. Everything He was, was all the Father is.... The only secret to the quality of life [Jesus] displayed was the Father living in the Son, without whom He could do nothing...[John 5:19]. So if you had gone to the Lord Jesus and said, "How did you feed the 5,000 with five loaves and two fishes?" the Lord Jesus would have said, "I didn't." [If you had said,] "Well, how did you raise Lazarus from the dead?" the Lord Jesus would have said, "I didn't." [If you had said,] "Well, how did you preach that magnificent Sermon on the Mount and give the world the beatitudes?" the Lord Jesus would have said, "I didn't... [and] oh, by the way, as I without My Father can do nothing, without me you can do nothing." [John 15:5]

The Apostle Peter declares this same truth in Acts 2:22, when he says Jesus was "*a man* attested to you by God with miracles and wonders and signs, which *God performed through Him* in your midst." Paul echoes this when he too says Jesus was *a man*, and that He did not regard equality with God a thing to be grasped "but emptied Himself" (Phil. 2:6,7). Jesus emptied Himself of His deity and of reliance upon his own ingenuity to effect change. Thus He said, "The Son can do nothing of Himself, unless it is something He sees the Father doing, for whatever the Father does the Son also does in like manner. For the Father loves the Son, and shows Him all things that He Himself is doing." (John 5:19,20)

Part Nine

Pictures of Paradigms:
How Heart Identities &
Giftings Can Meet in Real Life

Todd: A Wounded Son[26]

Todd's motivational gift is compassion. He also scores high in the area of serving. From a young age, Todd had a soft and spiritually sensitive heart with a sincere and unwavering desire to serve God. His extended family is brimming with men who are pastors, and mothers and wives who take comfort in knowing they are pastors. Todd's father is a prominent church board member. His mother is active in children's ministry and several other church-related functions.

As a teenager, Todd determined that after high school he would head for Bible college. Using student loans and income from part-time jobs, he obtained a degree in biblical studies. Shortly thereafter, a rather large congregation offered him a position as an assistant youth pastor. He accepted, and very quickly his genuine love for troubled teens shone through in a way that the kids recognized.

He effectively ministered to young people who struggled with personal insecurities, dysfunctional families, and addictions. He was especially effective in one-on-one situations and small groups.

Some months later, the senior youth pastor resigned and a new youth pastor was needed. Knowing Todd was doing well with troubled kids, the executive pastor approached him. Todd was too inexperienced to realize that there is an important distinction between a church office or job title and the actual expression of ministry. Nor did he fully appreciate that the position he was being offered had more to do with program maintenance than the one-on-one ministry he loved and at which he was so effective.

The church's executive pastor who offered Todd the position was a keen and seasoned administrator who, unfortunately, had the heart identity of a Laborer. As an administrator, his approach to ministry was to think in terms of planning, budgets, and program maintenance. As a Laborer, he measured success in the youth department by attendance and the number of events available. Todd, who had the heart identity of a Son, viewed success in terms of the lasting impact he could have on individual kids. His desire was to show compassion to them, but the responsibilities in his job description called for the development and maintenance of programs.

Almost immediately, frustration began to set in. On several occasions, Todd felt the need to resign, but each time he did, he struggled, asking himself how he could abandon the ministry he had thought about and planned for all his life. The executive pastor, assuming Todd's internal struggle was due to inexperience, encouraged him to hang in there. "The kids need a leader," he would say. Every time he said it, Todd would cringe and become even more troubled. He didn't aspire to be a leader. He wanted to show compassion by relieving the hurt of these kids and expressing kindness to them.

Two years later, deeply discouraged by his inability to expand programs and draw a crowd, struggling with student loans and what had become a troubled marriage, Todd resigned and left the church. His despair and sense of failure were thorough and complete. Today, Todd works as a tradesman on construction sites riddled with people whose lives are characterized by addictions and broken marriages. He has found the perfect place to minister. Some days, Todd still suffers from the mistaken belief that he was a failure. Yet with a small group of troubled kids, he was remarkably effective, especially in one-on-one counseling situations. Through Todd, several young people received the help they needed to overcome addictions and realign their lives.

Years later, the man who took over the position of youth pastor after Todd had left approached him to ask forgiveness. He confessed that rather harsh things had been said about Todd and his lack of success, especially after he himself succeeded in putting together a youth program that drew hundreds of young people on a weekly basis. It had taken him several years to realize that the kids Todd had ministered to were more stable and going on with the Lord, while the kids he was attracting with programs and weekend light shows were primarily involved for the entertainment value. When the entertainment stopped, the kids he attracted wandered off. When the entertainment stopped, the kids Todd had ministered to kept right on walking with God.

Audrey and Joyce

Audrey has a perceiver gift, scores high in compassion, and has the heart identity of a Beggar. She sees herself as a victim. Though she is almost 40 years old, she has never been able to hold a job. She is a regular user of mood-altering drugs.

Audrey sees the world in terms of victims and villains. She believes men, corporations, organized religion, and capitalists are prone to be villains, while women, children, workers, and people of color are victims. She has a sister and two brothers. They grew up in a home headed by an alcoholic father who sexually abused Audrey and her sister Joyce. After her second divorce, fully aware she had been wounded as a child, Audrey decided her father was responsible not just for the wounds she had suffered in childhood, but for everything else she didn't like about the way her life was turning out. She began to seek out therapists who would spend hours listening to her restate the reasons she was the way she was. Only therapists who agreed with her self-diagnosis were considered professional enough to handle her situation.

Unable to afford the fee, Audrey presented the bill to her father, who some years earlier had gotten involved with Alcoholics Anonymous, reformed his life, and stopped drinking. "You made me the way I am," she accused, "Now you have to pay for what you created."

Audrey's sister Joyce, also abused by her father, today has the heart identity of a Daughter. Like her sister, she went through a season of deep internal struggles. But unlike Audrey, who concluded that her father was responsible for her life, her feelings, and all she had been denied as a child, Joyce humbled herself, which is the prerequisite to forgiveness. From her heart, Joyce forgave her father, and although it involved a long and painful process, she was nevertheless set free from the woundedness that had previously characterized her life. Today she is a happily married mother of three.

Blaming the Perceiver

Oliver has a perceiver gift and the heart identity of an Orphan. For many years, along with his wife Sally and four children, he attended a prominent evangelical church. Church life had been pretty predictable until the leaders of the congregation decided church growth would become a dominant theme. To that end, the pastor and elders began to implement a plan they believed would facilitate what they envisioned. Instinctively recognizing that problems could arise because of the way they were going about it, Oliver verbalized his thoughts at church business and membership meetings. Initially, the church leadership thanked Oliver for his comments and responded in a gracious manner. When Oliver realized his comments were heard, but not considered, he continued vocalizing them, even stepping up the volume. He knew he could see something that the pastor and church board didn't seem to be able to recognize.

Confident in their plan for growth, the church leadership began to think Oliver had trouble with authority. Some leaders eventually labeled him as a somewhat sour individual who, for some reason they couldn't understand, decided to be negative about the "good things" they were trying to do. They simply kept telling him that he should be supportive rather than critical.

A few other members of the congregation who shared Oliver's perceiver gift understood exactly what he was talking about. They shared his concern, and a small group of them asked if there might be a way to have Oliver's name added to the board of elders. They wanted to add what they believed to be his insightful perspective to the overall leadership structure. Without considering the consequences, or even realizing what was happening, members of the congregation began drifting into factions, one supporting Oliver's position and the other supporting the leaders. The day eventually arrived when it was announced at a church staff meeting that Oliver was "dangerous" to the congregation's well-being.

THE MEETING OF PARADIGMS

As tension mounted, Oliver realized the implications of what was happening, and upon reflection, concluded the best way to diffuse the situation would be for him and Sally to find another fellowship. The implications were awkward. They had attended the congregation for many years. They had adult children and grandchildren who attended. Some of their friendships ran deep. The result was that as soon as they departed, family members and friends felt forced to choose between loyalty to church leadership and their plan, and their relationship with Oliver and Sally.

Time has proven Oliver's original observations to be quite valid. Yet, years later, many of the fractured relationships remain unreconciled.

Chandra's Struggle

Barry has a perceiver gift and is an exhorter. Barry's wife, Adele, also has a perceiver gift and scores high as an administrator. They have three children, two of whom have perceiver gifts. The youngest child, Chandra, was born with an exhortation gift and also scores high in the area of administration.

At the family dinner table, Barry relished discussing issues of insight, as did his wife and two older children. In their home, the assessment of politics, culture, and questions of theology occurred on a daily basis. The two older children are now extremely perceptive adults, having spent hundreds of hours discussing issues of insight with their mother and father.

During the daily family discourse, Chandra never had much to say. In an attempt to draw her into the discussions, Barry would turn to her and ask her opinion. She would shrug and add little.

She didn't dare tell him that she didn't understand half of what was being talked about, or that she feared saying something stupid. Not understanding that she was incapable of entering into the discussion with the same insight as her brother and sister, Barry made repeated attempts to get her to do so, which fostered and fed a struggle within her. The inability of Chandra's family, and especially her father, to understand the unique nature of her giftedness hurt her.

Chandra's struggle was compounded by the fact that Barry was a man with the heart identity of a Laborer. He viewed knowhow and ability as a means to "achieve for God." Relishing such things, he found his identity in them. Chandra, on the other hand, was reluctant even to think in such terms. She longed to be accepted for who she was rather than what she might achieve or know how to do.

As a teenager, behind her usual smile, Chandra began seeing herself not for who she was but who she was not. She began to struggle with thoughts of suicide, even after she finished high school and left home. Wisely, she sought out a Christian counselor who helped her work through some of her feelings.

Today, Chandra, a mother of three small children, understands and appreciates the nature of her own unique giftedness. Her father came to understand the consequences of his actions and how unfair he had been with her. Though he still lives with sorrow over what he did to hurt the daughter he loves, he and Chandra are in the process of building a healthy relationship.

. . . .

146

Anton's Quest for Approval

Anton has the heart identity of an Orphan. He is a kind man, about 30 years old, who registered to attend a series of classes at his church on the subject of motivational gifts. Halfway through the first class, during a short break, he approached the instructor to discuss a career decision he was about to make. Within the next few days, he intended to quit his position as a janitor in order to enroll in university. He was going to become a teacher.

When the instructor asked why, Anton replied that from the time he was a youngster, his mother had spoken of his need to be a professional. She constantly suggested he become a teacher, spoke fondly of teachers, and always said they did better in life than non-professionals. Anton also knew that his mother was somewhat ashamed of what he did for a living, and he wanted her approval.

Anton also told the instructor that his wife had abandoned him the previous year, and that he believed this was due to his lack of a professional career. In his heart, he was afraid that if he didn't become a professional, and if he ever married again, his future wife might leave him for the same reason. He believed graduating with a degree in teaching would protect him from disapproval and abandonment.

Several hours later, after working his way through the seminar's evaluation instrument, a tool designed to identify and explain a person's area of giftedness, Anton again spoke with the instructor. He had scored highest in serving and compassion. His lowest scores were in the areas of teaching and exhortation.

Rather than making a statement about Anton's intention to become a teacher, the session instructor asked him if he enjoyed working at his current job. Anton said that he absolutely loved it. Every day he was able to interact with people in a casual setting and meet their needs. People were not threatened by a janitor, and were willing to listen to a kind word he might speak to them. He felt he was able to minister to them and that many doors were open to him.

Asked how he felt about the prospect of standing in front of people to teach, Anton replied he was pretty nervous about the idea, but was sure the university would teach him how to do it. Asked if he enjoyed reading and studying books, he said no. The instructor then went over the evaluation instrument with him, pointing out that Anton had scored highest in serving and compassion. He suggested Anton would be happiest and most effective in a profession calling for those two areas of giftedness, perhaps in the area of health care. It was the first time it had ever occurred to Anton that his area of giftedness could match his vocation. He left the seminar promising he would prayerfully consider what he had learned.

Many months later, the instructor received an email from Anton, in which Anton repeatedly thanked him for pointing out that he would be happiest if he submitted himself to God and sought a career matching his giftedness. Previously, Anton had falsely believed that to gain approval he had to be different from the way he really was.

Six months after the seminar, Anton said he had indeed submitted himself and his gifting to God. A realignment in his heart was occurring. He felt comfortable in his own skin for the first time in his life. He was beginning to think like a Son, rather than an Orphan. He now believed the Father had placed him in the janitorial position he held in order to minister to the needs of people and to have an open door into their lives to bless them.

Gene Finds Identity in "Busyness"

Gene is a relatively new Christian. He has the Romans 12 gift of serving and the heart identity of a Laborer. His skill with electronics, mechanics, gardening, and home repairs puts him in high demand. Other people are aware of his disposition and find no end of activities for him. Gene can't say no to any of it, and doesn't want to. He derives a sense of satisfaction from doing such things, and relishes it when people tell him how much he has helped.

When Gene helps, he feels like he is being himself. He is also attracted to serving in the church because he mistakenly believes ministry takes place only within the context of the institution, and that God is pleased with him when he helps out around the building or at the homes of church members.

While Gene is finding fulfillment by meeting needs within the institutional church, resentment is brewing at home. His wife believes he is ignoring her and their practical needs. She thinks Gene is so busy doing church work that he has lost touch with non-believing neighbors, friends, and family. Gene, who equates his "busyness" with spirituality and pleasing God, thinks his wife has a rebellious attitude toward church and church activities.

. . . .

Peter and Warren

Peter is a perceiver/exhorter with the heart identity of a Son. His wife Gwen is a perceiver with the heart identity of a Daughter. For several years, Peter and Gwen attended a church with a congregation of about 400.

Their pastor, a man named Warren, had taught business and administration at a local community college before coming to Christ. In addition to having a teaching gift, he scores high as an administrator. He has the heart identity of a Laborer. One evening, Pastor Warren and his wife invited Peter and Gwen to their home for tea. They wanted to talk with them about their role in the church. "You have fruitful lives," Warren said. "I can see it. But all the fruit seems beyond my reach. When are you going to get out of the stands and get on the playing field?" That evening, Peter and Gwen received a rebuking for their lack of involvement in the church. The pastor didn't criticize their attendance record or their giving. They had been givers and rarely missed a service. He was critical because he didn't believe they were engaged in a way that would make them as influential as they could be. Peter and Gwen had led a weekly Bible study and served on several church committees, but Warren was convinced the two of them could do much more.

As Peter and Gwen made their way home that evening, somewhat stinging from the rebuke, they had to admit that what Pastor Warren had said was true. They could be more influential if they took on a more formal and deliberate leadership role. The next day, Peter contacted Warren, saying that he and Gwen had agreed with his assessment. It was decided that Peter and Gwen should begin their new involvement by taking over the youth ministry. What took place next was a colossal clash of paradigms—a clash of giftings and of heart identities.

As a perceiver, Peter's first step in understanding his new role was to learn how the young people were supposed to fit into the church's overall ministry, place in the community, and long-term vision. As such, Peter approached Warren and asked him to explain his God-given vision for the church. Warren, a teacher/administrator with the heart identity of a Laborer, had always assumed the role of a local church was to maintain vibrant programs, and expand them, thus attracting more people.

Peter intuitively sensed there was a great difference between a God-given vision for a ministry or church, and the desire to expand a program or add a new one. As a result, when Warren responded to his inquiry by talking vaguely about "taking the city for God" and listing a menu of program options, Peter felt his question was unanswered. Wanting to submit himself to the pastor's earlier rebuke, and believing the only way he could do so would be to understand, and then help implement, Warren's God-given vision for the congregation, he kept pressing him for an answer.

In time, Peter began to put forward possibilities, asking Pastor Warren if *this* or *that* was what his God-given vision for the church might be. Warren, unable to fully comprehend what Peter was asking, and therefore unable to provide him with an answer, began to make guesses in return—guesses that were formed within the context of his heart identity as a Laborer and gifting as a teacher/administrator. He began to speculate about why Peter kept asking him in the first place. With each passing week, discussions between Peter and Warren became increasingly focused, and eventually grew tense. Warren finally concluded Peter's questions were nothing more than criticism of himself as a leader, and of his leadership style. Deeply wounded, he told Peter how much he regretted letting him get close to him and his wife, saying that Peter's motive for his pointed questioning was undoubtedly rooted in ambition and rebellion. He then suggested that Peter's behavior probably had something to do with the fact that he had never been invited to sit on the church's board of directors.

Not saying anything to anyone in the congregation about what had transpired between the two men, and believing there to be no opportunity to submit to the pastor's initial rebuke apart from familiarity with his God-given vision, Peter and Gwen resigned as leaders of the youth ministry, left the congregation, and sought Christian fellowship elsewhere. Shortly thereafter, Peter's office transferred him to a branch in another city. Warren still pastors the same congregation. It has expanded its program options and experienced growth in attendance.

Part Ten

More Implications on Leadership

Sons and Daughters as Leaders

Hudson Taylor founded a missionary society that had a deep and lasting impact on millions of Chinese scattered across several generations. His vision was born in the barrenness of a human soul experiencing intense need and great spiritual agony. Taylor deliberately refused to construct with his hands what God did not breathe into his heart, and in humility, submitted his condition of spiritual poverty to the Holy Spirit (Matt. 5:3). As a result, his life became a healthy, open, and empty womb, ready to receive the seed of life that originates from the Father.

Taylor's vision was Spirit-born on a quiet Sunday morning while he was on furlough from China, staying at the Pearse family home on the English coast. While the tide was out, he took the opportunity to walk along the smooth sand left in its wake.

Heart-wrenching obstacles and conflict in his personal life were tearing at his soul. In addition, he was physically ill. Responding in prayer and humility, mourning his admitted barrenness, he continued seeking God, and it was there upon the sand that the Lord met him. As a result, the vision for the China Inland Mission was born. In writing about his experience some years later, Taylor said:

> "How restfully I turned away from the sands. The conflict ended, all was joy and peace. I felt as if I could fly up the hill to [the] Pearse house. And how I did sleep that night!" [27]

Two days later, Taylor opened a bank account in the name of the China Inland Mission. This was the first appearance of the name that would become familiar to so many.[28]

Pastors and church leaders with the heart identity of Sons and Daughters are alive and well in the 21st century. One example is Richard Sanchez. Richard is 75 years old, semi-retired, and lives on the west coast with his wife of 53 years. He spent 51 of those years as pastor at several different congregations.

Richard's motivational gifts are compassion and teaching, and because of the humility of his heart, he has never lost sight of his limitations. Whenever a church board or search committee would try to hire Richard, he would smile peacefully and say pleasantly to them, "If you're looking for some kind of Joshua to lead this congregation, I'm not the person. I don't do well with administrative details. If you're looking for someone to handle those things, you'll have to hire another person. I'm not interested in trying to lead this church into anything. My gifts are pastoring and teaching. I'll spend my time in prayer and the Word. God will give me my daily assignments. I'll have lunch with the administrator once a week. He can tell me whatever I need to know, and I'll tell him I'll see him on Sunday."

Anyone who heard Richard's sermons knew he always spoke of the deeper life. He never laid out a how-to plan. All he talked about was having a more intimate relationship with God, and abiding in Him. He always worked relationally with people. This was his gift, and he knew it. The people of the congregation always felt that Richard loved and cared for them, and as they listened to him speak of the things God birthed into his life, they found their own relationship with God growing deeper and more fruitful.

Some pastors would speak disparagingly of Richard, saying he lived in a different dimension from them. Richard was simply not interested in the things they were interested in. While they attended conferences on church growth and busied themselves with programs, Richard would spend time alone with God, or meet with members of his congregation one-on-one as God led him.

Other pastors, exhausted and near the point of burnout, would marvel at Richard's apparent ability to hold a church together and would try to recruit him to "be part of our team." Richard was never interested. He was not ambitious for success in the way many of his colleagues defined it. The paradigm of a Son, which defined his life, didn't even permit him to think in terms of trying to be successful.

Richard recently noted that although he was pastor at some rather large congregations, he never burned out and never sacrificed his family for the work of the church. He kept his motivational gift and his ministry gift in perspective. Today, he accepts short-term appointments where he teaches and preaches for two or three months at a time while a congregation is going through a transition in leadership. Throughout his life, he has been used by God to draw thousands of people into a more intimate Son/Daughter relationship with the Father.

The reason Richard Sanchez has been able to live free from ambition and the quest to succeed is that his identity is rooted in the identity of his Father. He understands how utterly dependent he is upon the Father for everything he needs and does. The humility of heart that characterizes his life makes him able to live as a Son.

Though men like Richard Sanchez occupy a specific role in the organic, Christ-centered church (as opposed to the institutional church), it is important to remember that their role is not an *exclusive* one. In the Christ-centered church there is no distinction between clergy and laity (I Pet. 2:9; Rev. 1:5,6). And no matter what our role or gifting may be, we are the Sons and Daughters of our Eternal Father.

But when the fullness of the time came, God sent forth His Son, born of a woman, born under the Law, in order that He might redeem those who are under the Law, that we might receive the adoption as sons. And because you are sons, God has sent forth the Spirit of His Son into our hearts, crying "Abba! Father!" Therefore you are no longer a slave, but a son... (Gal. 4:4-7)

Prayer

Father, thank You that You have called me to be Your Son/Daughter. I pray that by Your Holy Spirit, You will work in me a greater understanding of Your ways; that I might discern between what is born of You and what is born of my own desire and understanding; that Your Spirit would realign my heart so I can more fully know fellowship with You, hear Your voice, abide in Your presence, and walk in Your ways.

Father, Your Son Jesus taught that the Kingdom of Heaven belongs to those who are poor in spirit. Keep me from self-sufficiency, and grant that I will have the disposition and humility of heart not to attempt to escape the barrenness and spiritual poverty of my own soul, but to submit to You in the midst of it, looking to your Spirit to birth in me, and kindle in me, the heart identity and disposition of a Son/Daughter.

I pray that You will grant that what I see for the future will not be limited or defined by my past, nor by assumptions I may not even know I make about You, myself, or the nature of Christian service and ministry. Free me from pride, even hidden pride. Deliver me from false paradigms and, by your Spirit, enable me to live and walk as the Son/Daughter You have called me to be. I ask these things of You in the name of Your Son, Jesus Christ. Amen.

Notes

1. John White, *Changing on the Inside* (Guildford, Surrey, UK: Eagle, 1991) 53-54.

2. Joel Barker, *Paradigms: The Business of Discovering the Future* (New York: Harper Business, 1992) 15-19. The information presented here is based upon the historic data and text presented by Barker in this interesting volume.

3. *The Final Countdown*, Dir. Don Taylor, Lion's Gate Films, 1988.

4. Elsewhere in Scripture and depending upon the translation, the Hebrew word rendered "springs" in this passage is translated "outgoing," "border," "issues," or "forth." If a person used the word "border" in a conversation about geography, he would be speaking about a boundary. In the KJV, the passage says that out of the heart flow the "issues" of life. To "issue" means to "send or give out." For example, police officers issue speeding tickets and traffic citations, government mints issue currency, and the July publication of a monthly magazine is called the July issue. The "issues" of life that spring from our hearts are the things that reveal who and what we are.

5. The passage literally reads: "I have declared that which I did not understand, things too wonderful for me, which I did not know. Hear now and I will speak; I will ask You, and You instruct me. I have heard of you by the hearing of the ear; but now my eye sees You; Therefore I retract, and I repent in dust and ashes." (Job 42:3-6 NASB)

6. This is not to imply that Beggars are the only people who suffer from addictions, but to recognize that the circumstances of their lives can make them especially prone to medicants.

7. Please see "Acknowledgements, Credits, and Sources" to understand the role of Francis Frangipane and Becky Avram in the development of the material in "Part Six: The Heart Identity of a Son or Daughter."

8. John MacArthur, *Hard to Believe* (Nashville: Thomas Nelson Publishers, 2003) 83-84.

9. Stated by Francis Frangipane, in an interview for the *This is Your Day* program. Francis was teaching on the steps to holiness in Matthew 5.

10. *Ibid.*

11. *Ibid.*

12. *Ibid.*

13. Eugene Peterson, quoted in John White, *Changing on the Inside* (Guildford, Surrey, UK: Eagle, 1991) 89-91. The text presented here is a paraphrase of that which White attributes to Peterson.

14. Stated by Francis Frangipane, in an interview for the *This is Your Day* program. Francis was teaching on the steps to holiness in Matthew 5.

15. *Ibid.*

16. *Ibid.*

17. *Ibid.*

18. *Ibid.*

19. *Ibid.*

20. The Greek word used here is *proistemi*, which means "to superintend" or "preside over." Elsewhere in Scripture, and depending upon the translation, it is also rendered "maintain," "lead," "rule," "manage," "engage," and "give aid." For ease of use and

to avoid any suggestion that this motivational gift competes with the ministry gifts of Ephesians 4:11, we use the modern English word "administration."

21. John 1:13 makes it clear that there are four distinct sources that give rise to the process of "giving birth": blood, the will of the flesh, the will of man, and God.

22. Major Ian Thomas is a well-known Bible teacher and founder of Torchbearers International— www.torchbearers.gospelcom.net/.

23. The many "people stories" presented in this volume are based on actual events. However, in order to draw attention to circumstances and contrasts rather than personalities, names have been changed as well as certain details.

24. Dr. James Stone's website and study material can be accessed via the web at: www.wayofchrist.org.

25. Major Ian Thomas is a well-known Bible teacher and founder of Torchbearers International— www.torchbearers.gospelcom.net/.

26. The many "people stories" presented in this volume are based on actual events. However, in order to draw attention to circumstances and contrasts rather than personalities, names have been changed as well as certain details.

27. Dr. & Mrs. Howard Taylor, *A Biography of James Hudson Taylor* (London: Hodder & Stoughton, 1997) 235-236.

28. *Ibid.*

For further understanding of the beatitudes, see Francis Frangipane's material on the subject at:
www.arrowbookstore.com

Acknowledgements, Credits, and Sources

It is sometimes difficult to define when or from whom a person learns things. Sometimes the Father reveals things to us in the quietness of our own hearts. At other times, a pastor, teacher, or prophetic minister may be teaching when the Holy Spirit opens our heart, and rather than being spoken to by that man or woman, we are taught by God. At such a time, hearing the Spirit apply truth to our hearts doesn't just change what we know or how we behave, it changes who we are.

With respect to the manuscript and publication, there are three individuals we must acknowledge: The first two are Helen Edwards and Christa Bonnell. Helen was instrumental in helping us connect some of the early thoughts. The first few times we met with her, we believed we were simply putting together a series of individual papers to post on a website. She asked the challenging questions, wanted to know why we thought or said certain things, and ensured we stayed focused. Christa helped with the layout, on several occasions went through the manuscript with us line by line, and suggested many insightful changes or possibilities. The third person who took our hand was Lila Nelson at Arrow Publications. Lila proofed the manuscript, mothered us through dozens of details, and did it all with such grace and professionalism. We are grateful for the contribution made by each of these women.

Kevin Avram: In the past 10 years, there are two people the Father used to facilitate the realignment of heart that led to my role in this book and at Foundations of Purpose. The first is Francis Frangipane—an author, book publisher, teacher, and pastor at River of Life Church in Cedar Rapids, Iowa. Some years ago, Francis conducted a teaching on the steps to holiness, using Matthew 5 as his text. The impact of that teaching upon my life was profound, and can be seen in "Part Six: The Heart Identity of a Son or Daughter." As seen by the footnotes in this chapter, there are places where we have repeated concepts or phrases first learned from Francis's teaching. The heart identities of Laborers, Orphans, Beggars, and Sons/Daughters is a teaching the Father first revealed to my wife, Becky. She treasured it in her heart and began praying that the Lord would give me the heart identity of a Son. The Holy Spirit moved in ways she would never have imagined. As the manuscript unfolded, especially parts five and six, which articulate the characteristics of heart identity, handwritten notes from her personal prayer journal became a valuable resource.

Wes Boldt: Over a period of years, prior to working with Foundations of Purpose International, the Father kept leading me into situations where I could learn about motivational gifts and their characteristics. He taught me in the quietness of my personal study. I also learned through seminars, conferences, short-term schools, the writings of those who teach about the gifts and one-on-one meetings with them. The nature of this type of prolonged learning process makes it difficult to assign credit when and where appropriate, but to that end, I wish to acknowledge the valuable contribution made to my life by my friends Don and Katie Fortune at Heart 2 Heart Ministries.

Foundations of Purpose International

Kevin Avram and Wes Boldt serve with Foundations of Purpose International, a Christian ministry and service organization operating out of locations in Scottsdale, Arizona, and Sherwood Park, Alberta, Canada.

The role of Foundations of Purpose is to provide individuals, churches, and Christian ministries with the means to better understand the four distinct identities of the heart revealed in Scripture, their source, the impact they have upon relationships, and the manner in which they influence church and ministry structures. In addition, under the guidance of the Holy Spirit, Foundations of Purpose works to provide individual believers with a better understanding of how heart identity influences the way motivational and ministry gifts are expressed within those structures.

The ministry is available to participate in a variety of forums, including short-term projects working alongside church leaders and Christian ministries. In this context, the objective is to facilitate a better understanding of:

Power: "Not by might, not by power, but by My Spirit" (Zech. 4:6). Considering what power means, its various sources, the way it is expressed, and how leaders inadvertently use the levers of power to manipulate people and circumstances.

Heart Identity: God-given vision, heartfelt ambition, or an abiding sense of duty; understanding how the identity of the heart in leaders is manifested, and the influence it has upon the structure and culture of individual churches and Christian ministries.

Organizational Culture: The organizational culture in your church or ministry may be the most influential and valuable aspect of what you do. What is organizational culture? How is it nurtured or hindered? What happens when a leader tries to manipulate it rather than nurture it? What is the impact of organizational culture upon individuals, families, and the community?

Corporate Will: Every organizational structure, including churches and Christian ministries, expresses a will. What is corporate will? How does it differ from the will of the leader? How is corporate will determined and expressed? What is its impact?

Identity and Purpose: The consequence when a church or Christian ministry fails to differentiate between its identity, its purpose, and its activities.

Purpose and Values: Why there is a tendency for many Christian leaders to mistakenly assume purpose and values are synonymous, and the unfortunate fallout that occurs when they conclude they are.

Structures: Organic life is characterized by structure, so are bureaucracies. Knowing the difference, and understanding the factors that inhibit, permit, or nurture.

Burnout: Why the ministry is rated one of the top risks for burnout by some insurance companies and what to do about it.

Ministry Gifts: The implications when leaders overlook or fail to recognize the sometimes subtle but far-reaching distinction between ministries ordained of God or offices with corporate responsibilities designated by government.

Workplace Inventories: Providing churches and ministries with testing instruments that accurately demonstrate the practical outworking of motivational gifts and personal preferences in organizational settings and strategic undertakings.

FOUNDATIONS OF PURPOSE INTERNATIONAL
Website: www.foundationsofpurpose.org
Email: contact@foundationsofpurpose.org

Also available from Jon Zens...

The Pastor Has No Clothes!
Moving From Clergy-Centered Church to Christ-Centered Ekklesia
(Spring 2011)

What's With Paul And Women?
Unlocking the Cultural Background to 1 Timothy 2
(2010)

A Church Building Every 1/2 Mile
What Makes American Christianity Tick?
(2008)

PRE-EKKLESIA PUBLISHED

"This Is My Beloved Son, Hear Him":
The Foundation for New Covenant Ethics & Ecclesiology
Searching Together, 1997

Moses & the Millennium:
An Appraisal of Christian Reconstructionism
Searching Together, 1988

Desiring Unity...Finding Division:
Lessons from the 19th Century Restorationist Movement
Searching Together, 1986

The above are available at www.jonzens.com

Agreeing with Jon Zens in his passionate pursuit of God's kingdom and righteousness, I can heartily endorse his plea for justice as it pertains to gender issues. "There is neither male nor female; for you are all one in Christ Jesus." Regardless of the depth and nature of abuse, it has no place in the new creation.

— **Don Atkin**, author of *Creation's Cry*

I concur completely with the observations in *No Will of My Own*. As I read it, discomfort, sorrow and memories of those girls I've either counseled or known in the church who have suffered abuse flooded my mind. Anything I can do to assist a wide distribution of a book containing these painful truths I would be glad to do. Obviously, I believe that the more exposure of the tragedy of both patriarchal theology and the crime of the abuse of women, the better.

— **Greg Austin**, WA

In almost every religion around the world, the hearts, souls, and bodies of women are sacrificed on the altar of fundamentalism. In *No Will of My Own*, Jon Zens takes a sobering look at abuse within patriarchal Christianity. An important book.

— **Hillary McFarland**, author of *Quivering Daughters: Hope and Healing for the Daughters of Patriarchy*

There can be no doubt that the Christian patriarchy movement is growing and influencing mainstream evangelicalism, ushering in a new doctrine of father/daughter relationships that has no basis in the Word of God. Should we be surprised to see that such a system of control, domination, and spiritual abuse can foster an environment for potential sexual abuse as well? Thankfully, in *No Will of My Own*, author and women's advocate, Jon Zens, has given us an opportunity to examine some of the fruits of this movement and has called us to action. I pray that the church will listen.

— **Karen Campbell**, author and creator of Thatmom Podcasts at www.thatmom.com

In *No Will of My Own*, Jon Zens summarizes the personal and material toll patriarchy takes on its most submissive participants. By robbing women of their voice and their personhood, so-called "Christian" patriarchy leaves them with nothing to submit with! These women are beautiful but passive, adoring but absent. This ideology's appeal to men is obvious: it acts like a kind of domesticated pornography—a living portrayal of sexual dominance for the purposes of egocentric excitement and satisfaction.

Having studied the rhetoric of religious separatists and their attempt to woo others toward their ethic at all costs, I know well their metanarrative of Romance. Jon vividly shows this metanarrative's destructive consequences. I hope every believer, both in the pew and in the pulpit, will read Zens' evidence with their eyes wide open to the sinful consequences of male-dominated and Christless hierarchies.

— **Camille Kaminski Lewis**, Ph.D., Independent Scholar, Author of *Romancing the Difference: Kenneth Burke, Bob Jones University, and the Rhetoric of Religious Fundamentalism*

Of the many chains that bind the human heart perhaps the most grievous are those that deny personhood. Denial of one's personhood is not only immoral; it is utterly antithetical to the work of grace God has wrought in the world through His loving plan of redemption. Whether the rationale for this denial is race, status, or gender, the result is the same: alienation in place of communion, abuse instead of healing, and misery in the place of wholeness. What Jon Zens does to expose the elusive lies and religious fallacies of patriarchy's chains is commendable. The research, insight, and wisdom found in this small book is life-giving, and in his own indomitable style the author offers a strong and assuring hand to those whose lives need it most.

— **Dr. Stephanie Bennett,** Associate Professor of Communication & Media Studies, Palm Beach Atlantic University

The Church has suffered from centuries of repugnant, ignorant, culturally biased, pagan, and misogynist values that misrepresent Paul. These values masquerade as faithfulness to the Scripture as a bulwark against the perceived encroachment of "liberalism" regarding gender issues. Jesus said: "By their fruit you will know them." Jon Zens' comprehensive work documents the aberrant and abusive fruit of fundamentalist patriarchy. Jon faithfully exposes the wide-spread, dark, and deeply disturbing hidden "under-belly" of gender-biased fundamentalism, which I have also experienced first hand. I pray that the Holy Spirit will set tens of thousands of daughters free through this book.

— **Dr. Stephen R. Crosby**, author of *The Silent Killers of Faith: Overcoming Legalism and Performance-Based Religion*

In *No Will of My Own*, Jon Zens challenges us to examine a frightening but logical, and authentic end result of living under patriarchal Christianity. His conclusions are shocking, sound, and well documented. I applaud him for his courage and thank him for this invaluable resource.

— **Jocelyn Andersen**, author of, *Woman this is WAR! Gender, Slavery & the Evangelical Caste System*

Too often, the church avoids painful discussions of unpleasant topics, especially those which take place within its own circles. *No Will of My Own* brings the heart-wrenching consequences of idolatrous patriarchy out of the darkness and into the light. Jon Zens graciously contrasts the insidious ideas that prop up the pagan practice with Biblical and common-sense truth, offering healing encouragement to the wounded. As the issues of gender and priestcraft pose some of the most significant challenges faced by today's Evangelical Church, his vital treatise proves both powerful and timely.

— **Cynthia Kunsman**, of
www.UnderMuchGrace.com and
the Freedom for Christian Women Coalition

Jon Zens can be contacted at:
jzens@searchingtogether.org or 715-338-2796

NO WILL OF MY OWN